Casablanca Cuisine

ALINE BENAYOUN was born and brought up in Casablanca and later in the South of France; she now lives in London. *Casablanca Cuisine* is her first book.

Casablanca Cuisine

FRENCH NORTH AFRICAN COOKING

Aline Benayoun

Decorations by Benedicte Barford

Serif

London

First published 1998 by
Serif
47 Strahan Road
London E3 5DA

British Library Cataloguing-in-Publication Data. A catalogue record for
this book is available from the British Library.

Library of Congress Cataloging in Publication Data. A catalog record
for this book is available from the Library of Congress.

ISBN 1 897959 33 8

Designed by Sue Lamble
Printed and bound in Ireland by ColourBooks, Dublin

Contents

To my parents, my husband and my children

avec tout mon amour

Acknowledgements

I WAS FORTUNATE in that I was able to collect many of the recipes in this book from my mother, Joséphine, who had learned how to cook them from her mother, Marie. What she wasn't able to give me, I managed to get from several aunts, including one who still lives in Casablanca. Other recipes came from my sisters – Gladys, Maryse and Joëlle.

Like so many hand-me-downs, alterations were necessary. We don't cook today in the West the way my grandmothers did in North Africa. For one thing, we don't have the time. Another problem was that my grandmothers, my aunts and even my mother never cooked with numbers – none of them could say how many tablespoons of this or grams of that went into a dish – because they always cooked with their eyes. They knew when it looked right and knew when it felt right and knew how to make it taste right. So I needed to sit down and watch while my mother cooked, and then I cooked all these dishes again to make certain that the numbers are right. My family's waistlines will never be the same.

Many thanks to Jessie, my mother-in-law, for her unfailing and enthusiastic encouragement, my brother Patrick and, as well, to Stephen Hayward at Serif. Right from the beginning, he understood what a special cuisine this is.

Introduction

THE FRENCH COLONISED North Africa at the end of the nineteenth and beginning of the twentieth century, and those of us who were born there are known as *pieds noirs* – 'black feet' – an expression apparently derived from the amazement of the sandal-wearing Arabs as they watched French soldiers landing on their shores wearing highly polished military boots.

The immigration that followed was not exclusively French. There were Italians, who went to Tunisia and the eastern part of Algeria, and Spaniards, who settled in Morocco or the western half of Algeria, and then, of course, there were the ruling French, who spread themselves over all three lands. The result was the creation, out of this melting-pot, of a new breed of Frenchman – the *pied noir* – a Frenchman who, in many cases, had never been to France.

North Africa was also home to the Sephardim, descendants of the Jews expelled from Spain and Portugal at the end of the fifteenth century. Morocco's Sephardim were concentrated above all in the cities of Fez and Marrakech and the port of Mogador, now known as Essaouira. They were kept apart from the broader Arab society by law, and when the French and other Europeans arrived they often identified with these new arrivals.

My own ancestors somehow made their way to Algeria from villages with unpronounceable names in the old Tsarist and Ottoman empires. Both my parents were born in Algeria as French citizens. For reasons now long forgotten, they had both moved with their parents to Casablanca, where they met and married, and where I was born.

'Casa', as we called it, was a sparkling white city on the Atlantic coast with wide avenues, tall palm trees, huge sandy beaches and wonderfully noisy, colourful markets. We spoke French, went to French schools and carried French passports. But for us, immersed as we were in such a glorious and resplendent Arab culture, France was far away – we referred to it as *la métropole* – the country on the other side of the Mediterranean where some of our great-grandparents had once lived. For us as children, France was hardly more than a place to visit on school holidays.

That is, until the early 1960s, when independence came to Morocco and we were forced to leave. We didn't have to suffer the horrors of war, as our *pied noir* cousins who lived in Algeria did, but it was clear that we were no longer welcome in Morocco, and the obvious thing to do was to 'return' to France. So we took whatever we could pack and left, tearfully, to resettle along the French Riviera, where the sea and the Mediterranean climate reminded us of home. I was just twelve when we left, and although I was raised in Antibes and now think of the Côte d'Azur as home, because we *pieds noirs* were bathed in an exotic tradition we remain very different from the rest of the French.

Nowhere is that difference more evident than in our cuisine. As rich in flavour as it is in history, our cooking was one of the few things we could take with us when we fled North Africa and almost half a century later that special cuisine is still handed down from mother to daughter. I have adapted my mother's and grandmother's recipes slightly for my own family, to meet today's different demands, but I have jealously guarded the aromatic combination of our multicultural roots – French, Spanish, Moroccan, Algerian, Tunisian and Sephardic, with a sprinkling of Italian influence. Naturally enough, Sephardic cooking followed Jewish dietary laws and had an impact on the *pieds noirs*, amongst whom there were, anyway, a number of Jews.

Traditionally based on the fresh ingredients which we could buy each morning in the market – both my grandmothers lectured me that a good meal begins in the markets – ours is a tasty and particularly healthy cuisine. Flavoured with spices such as saffron, paprika, chilli, cumin, coriander, cloves, cinnamon, nutmeg and allspice, most of the dishes are based on vegetables and fruit with light sauces.

At the same time, *pied noir* cooking is simple, requiring little more than basic kitchen skills. This makes it much more accessible than many of the cuisines recently 'discovered' by cooks in the West. Life in North Africa was, however, considerably slower than it is today in Europe and North America. My grandmothers had more time to cook, and *pied noir* cooking generally takes time. Patience, a virtue in the kitchen as elsewhere, will always be rewarded with a memorable meal.

✦✦✦✦✦

Unlike classical French cooking, *pied noir* cuisine is not known for elaborate desserts. Sweets were, and still are, brought out for tea and at weddings, family festivals and on religious holidays, but only rarely at the end of an ordinary meal. Cheese was served only very occasionally, as it isn't really suited to such a hot climate. Nevertheless, some French settlers continued to eat cheese even in the heat of North Africa and something of the French taste for cheese remained when we left. Today there are several good *fromageries* in Casablanca and cheese is served in some restaurants, but it was never an important part of our culinary tradition and hasn't really been taken up by the Moroccans. Neither will you find cream or butter in our cuisine, again because of the heat, and as a result our cooking is light and perfectly attuned to our health-conscious times.

What you can, however, always expect at the end of a *pied*

noir meal is fresh fruit – oranges, cantaloupe, apricots, peaches, watermelon – whatever is in season. The reason is obvious – fruit refreshes the palate and aids digestion. The final act in a *pied noir* meal is a glass of mint tea, a habit that we learned from the Arabs, of course. The tea is served as a natural complement to the fruit.

Another less definable element which we most definitely borrowed from our Arab neighbours and then made our own is a strong sense of hospitality. We believe that a great meal means more than just good food; it also means a table crowded with family and friends. If there is enough for eight, we reckon there is enough for nine, so we insist that friends of friends join us. And their friends are welcome too, because if there is enough for nine, then there is enough for ten.

We then surround our meal in conversation – which normally means several conversations at the same time and a helping of good-natured argument – and a constant nagging by the hostess that you haven't eaten enough. Nothing could possibly be more upsetting than to imagine someone might leave your table without feeling stuffed.

✦ ✦ ✦ ✦ ✦

We have a saying that every meal starts in the market, and in Morocco that means a morning visit to the *souk*. The markets were a pot-pourri of colour, noise, smells and constant movement, where the stalls were set up just after dawn. Serious shoppers got there early, knowing that the best produce went first and that the tourists would crowd you out by 10 o'clock.

I often accompanied my mother on her early-morning forays, mainly because I loved the theatre of the *souks*. I loved the general sense of abundance – the mountains of garlic, the baskets of lemons, the cascades of clear-eyed fish that had been in the sea only hours before. I loved the way whole families worked on the stalls, the grandfather mumbling to himself in the corner, the grandmother who ordered everyone around and the children getting in everyone's way by playing in the middle of the alleys. And I loved the old weighing scales onto which the sellers tossed everything, knowing in advance how many artichokes make a kilo, but still tipping the scales first in their favour and then, when you complained, adding an extra piece as if for free.

I loved being in the middle of the commotion: sellers shouting about their fruit; bragging about their vegetables; urging us to look at their meat and poultry; singing out, 'Sardines … tuna … sea bass … bream … squid … grouper … red mullet … sole …'; always promising that whatever they were hawking was cheaper than that sold by their cousin working on the next stall; haggling over the price until they swore that we were getting our food for less than they had paid for it.

It quickly became evident, hanging onto my mother's straw shopping basket as she moved through the markets, that there was method to her madness. She always walked first from one end of the *souk* to the other, quickly and without buying anything. It was almost as if she was going to meet someone at the far end and wasn't paying attention to any stall in particular. This was just her reconnaissance expedition and as her eyes darted from side to side she noted whose vegetables were the freshest and who had the best-looking fruit. Only after she had completed this ritual did she start shopping.

She would move from stall to stall, followed by one of the 'porters', a small boy who latched onto us to carry our shopping home in exchange for a small tip. She returned to those stalls whose produce she judged to be the best, taking care never to seem too anxious to buy what she actually wanted. First, she'd carefully inspect the produce, picking it up, squeezing it, smelling it. Then she would make a curious face, as if to say, 'Maybe this is alright, but I'm not really sure.' Finally, she would ask the price, knowing that it was already lower than the stall nextdoor and feigning surprise when the seller only offered her a small discount.

I would stand there wide-eyed, waiting for the stall-holder to hand me a small sample because, whenever possible, they always gave children a taste of whatever it was they were selling, as my mother began to haggle over the price. It wasn't until many years later that I understood this bargaining wasn't really about saving a few centimes, but an integral part of the culture, a rite that everyone took in their stride and a social function that united us with the Moroccan people. Unfortunately, when we left Morocco we discovered that this wasn't something which the French understood – the rules were different in *la métropole* and the pleasures of such a simple game had to be left behind. The French did not share our enthusiasm for bargaining and all too often rudely reminded us that the price was the price and that we were no longer in North Africa.

✦ ✦ ✦ ✦

The Arabs, of course, had been the world's leading spice merchants long before we arrived in North Africa and it was they who taught us how to flavour our food. Perhaps the most important lesson which we learned from them is that the freshness and variety of herbs and spices matter most, not the quantity, and as a result we always use a light hand when adding spices to a dish.

It used to be said that we could buy more than 300 different spices in the *souks* in North Africa, although I suspect that this figure is somewhat exaggerated. Almost all the spices were sold unground, piled into small heaps on the merchants' stands, creating a wonderful rainbow of colours and a tantalising array of aromas. Despite this abundance, spices were sold in very small quantities, normally just enough for the meal for which they were required, and the spice merchant would pour them into a small piece of paper which was then tightly wrapped.

My grandmothers always kept their spices wrapped in the paper in which they had bought them, and my mother still does so to this day, because they believed – and rightly so – that spices stored in glass jars are easily discoloured by sunlight and lose their flavour. The fashion for keeping spices on a kitchen shelf exposed to the light is the worst possible way of storing these expensive ingredients, which should be kept in a dark, dry cupboard.

Nowadays it is much easier to buy dried herbs and pre-ground spices and, although these keep quite well, there is a real difference in flavour, with fresh herbs giving much more aroma to a dish. Even today, I grow coriander, parsley and basil on my kitchen windowsill in central London.

Buying our spices this way meant that we ground them when we needed them, so a pestle and mortar were a permanent fixture on our kitchen table. Spices like cinnamon and cumin can often be bought whole in the West, and nothing could be easier than grinding them in an electric coffee-grinder. The resulting flavours are much sharper and more intense than those of the pre-ground varieties.

All too often people think that the word 'spicy' means hot, but this is not the case with our cuisine. We use certain spices, like turmeric, saffron and paprika, to give colour to a dish and others, like cumin, ginger, nutmeg and caraway, to create a particular flavour. And then we combine them to give both colour and flavour, as with the various recipes in this book which call for the typically *pied noir* combination of paprika and cumin.

✦✦✦✦✦

Cooking is one of the most important elements in Moroccan culture and has become so refined over the centuries that today the country's cuisine is widely considered to be the richest and most sophisticated in the Arab world. One reason for this is the country's geography. Although many Europeans and North Americans think of Morocco as a land of mountain and desert, much of the country is in fact very fertile and yields a great variety of produce, from olives and wheat to almonds and dates, from oranges and quinces to lemons and lamb. Moreover, it is the only Arab nation to be blessed with both Mediterranean and Atlantic coastlines.

The French turned Casablanca into one of North Africa's principal ports and an influential trading centre, and although Rabat is the capital, Casablanca is now Morocco's first city. Its Arab name is Dar El Beida – 'white house' – which was translated literally by eighteenth-century Spanish traders to Casablanca. Arabic is now the country's official language, but French is still widely spoken in Morocco. Our cultural roots were French, and to them we added Sephardic traditions and an appreciation and understanding of the customs of Islam.

The word Muslim means 'he who has accepted', referring, of course, to Allah. We are not Muslims, but a very strong family tradition lies at the heart of the *pied noir* way of life, just as it does in Moroccan culture. It is the mother who does the shopping, the mother who does the cooking and the mother who raises the children. The mother is, in short, the nucleus of the family, and it might well be this shared trait that formed the basis for the deep understanding which we as settlers shared with our native hosts.

For one month each year Muslims celebrate Ramadan, which requires them to fast all day. After sunset and the call to evening prayers at the mosque they return home for a family feast that begins with *harira*, a traditional soup made with vegetables, diced lamb, lentils, chick-peas, onion, parsley and coriander. It is one of the many recipes which we have borrowed from the Arabs, changed slightly and come to call our own. The line that separated us socially was very clearly drawn, but nevertheless certain aspects of our cultures blended into one another, and the best example of this is our cuisine, a unique hybrid of European, Arabic and Jewish ingredients and traditions, methods and influences.

La Kémia

THERE IS A RITUAL to eating *à la pied noir*. This starts with hors d'oeuvres, our equivalent of the Greek *mezze* or Spanish *tapas*, which we call *la kémia*.

After a brass pestle and mortar have been placed in the centre of the table for the shells and pits of the nuts and olives, the *anisette* appears. This is an aniseed-flavoured spirit that takes slightly different forms around the Mediterranean, as pastis in France and ouzo in Greece – you pour a small measure into the bottom of a glass, add a couple of ice cubes and then dilute it with cold water.

The pastis is accompanied by a table full of *amuse-gueule*, or palate-ticklers, small plates of dried fava beans, tiny spicy beef sausages called *merguez*, raw cauliflower florets and fennel, pistachio nuts, grilled almonds, hazelnuts, grilled watermelon seeds known as *pépites blanches*, chick-peas in cumin, pickles, several types of salami, liver pâté, fresh chillis, sardines cooked in garlic and vinegar, and large bowls of black, purple and green olives. Savoury preserves are also served as part of the *kémia*, and recipes for these are to be found in the chapter on preserves.

The origin of the word *kémia* is obscure, but my uncle's theory is that it comes from the Arabic word for smoking, which he pronounces *'kmeh'*. His idea, which is as persuasive as any of the theories which I've heard put forward, is that the expression comes from people's habit of meeting in cafés to smoke a cigarette, have a drink and nibble some snacks.

Beztels

MEAT IN FILO PASTRY

Preparation ✦ 30 minutes
Cooking ✦ 20 minutes
Makes about 24

12 sheets of filo pastry
250 g /8 oz minced beef
1 onion, chopped
1 egg
Juice of half a lemon
1 tbsp vegetable oil for browning the meat
Vegetable oil for deep-frying
A pinch of nutmeg
A pinch of allspice
Salt
Pepper

Filo pastry is difficult to make but, fortunately, can now be bought ready-made, either fresh or frozen, from almost all supermarkets.

To prepare the meat filling, heat the oil in a small pan, brown the onion and then add the meat, stirring until it too is brown. Season with salt, pepper, allspice, nutmeg and the lemon juice before adding half a pint of water. Cover the pan, reduce the heat and cook for 20 minutes.

Taking the pan off the heat, add the egg-yolk and mix it in while the meat is still hot. Now cut a sheet of filo pastry in half, put a tablespoon of the meat in the middle and fold it corner to corner to form a triangle.

Using a clean pan, heat vegetable oil (which should be about two inches deep) for deep-frying and cook the *beztels* until they turn a beautiful golden colour. Then transfer them onto kitchen paper to remove any excess oil before putting them in a serving dish.

Beztels can be eaten hot or cold, although I prefer them hot, and minced lamb can be substituted for the beef. My mother always makes more than she needs for any given meal, putting the extra *beztels* into the freezer, where they keep well.

Briks

EGGS IN FILO PASTRY

Preparation ✦ 3 minutes
Cooking ✦ 5 minutes
Makes 12

12 sheets of filo pastry
12 eggs
A bunch of fresh coriander
Salt
Pepper
Vegetable oil for deep-frying

Brik is usually considered a Tunisian speciality, as these packets of filo pastry are to be found there, filled with a great variety of stuffings, including a particularly tasty one of mashed potatoes, onion, parsley and olive oil. In Casablanca we tended to stick to the simple but classic version in which the *brik* contains a seasoned egg.

Making filo pastry is a tricky and time-consuming business, but it can now be bought ready-made in almost any supermarket and almost no one makes it at home any longer. Break one egg into each sheet of filo pastry, season with salt, pepper and chopped coriander, then carefully fold the pastry four times to make a small packet. This takes some practice because the egg will try to slip out! The best way is to fold the longer side first, then turn over the two smaller sides as flaps.

Heat the oil for deep-frying, fry until the *brik* is golden and serve immediately.

Fèves Sèches Frites

FRIED FAVA BEANS

Preparation ✦ 45 minutes
Cooking ✦ 30 minutes

1 kg / 2 lb dried fava beans, soaked overnight
Vegetable oil for frying
Salt
Pepper

Soak the fava beans overnight in cold water. After draining them, use a small knife to remove the skin and then open each bean, splitting them in two.

Heat the oil in a frying pan and, when it is almost smoking, pour in the beans and stir them until they're golden brown. Depending on the quantity and on the size of your frying pan, you may have to do this in batches. As soon as the beans are ready, remove them from the frying pan, taking care not to bring too much oil with the beans, and lay them out on a clean paper towel. Once they are slightly cooler, fold the towel in half and gently pat the top so as to soak up any remaining oil. Then put them to one side until they are completely cool.

To serve, put the beans in a small bowl and sprinkle them with salt and pepper. They're eaten like peanuts.

If you've made more beans than you need and want to store some, they keep well in a glass jar. But make sure not to salt and pepper them until you're actually ready to serve them, because if you store them already seasoned, they will be too soft when you come to eat them.

Pâté de Foie

LIVER PÂTÉ

Preparation ✦ 30 minutes
Cooking ✦ 30 minutes

750 g / 1½ lb calf's or lamb's liver, sliced
4 tbsp vegetable oil
2 large onions, finely chopped
1 carrot, chopped
1 bay leaf
Salt
Pepper

Lightly grill the slices of liver, rinse them and then cut them into 2 inch squares.

Heat the oil in a saucepan over a medium flame, add the

chopped onions, carrot, bay leaf, liver, salt, pepper and half a pint of water and cook, half-covered, for 30 minutes.

Reduce the heat, remove the lid from the saucepan and simmer, stirring frequently so that the liver and vegetable mixture doesn't burn, until there is no more liquid in the pan. Removing the bay leaf, empty the contents of the pan into a food-processor and mix until you have a smooth pâté. Allow to cool to room temperature before serving.

Méguéna

BRAIN PÂTÉ

Preparation ✦ 30 minutes
Cooking ✦ 1 hour

1 calf's brain
10 eggs
250 g/8 oz pre-cooked mixed vegetables
A bunch of parsley, chopped
1 Spanish onion, finely chopped
4 tbsp vegetable oil
1 tsp nutmeg
Salt
Pepper

Boil the brain in salted water for 10–15 minutes, wash it and cut it into 1½ inch cubes. While the brain is boiling, brown the onion in a saucepan with half the oil.

My grandmothers made this pâté with a mixture of vegetables (carrots, cauliflower florets, peas and so on) which they had prepared themselves, but they were accustomed to spending the entire day in the kitchen. Nowadays we tend to use pre-cooked rather than fresh vegetables for this part of the recipe – it's best to buy them in a glass jar so that you know exactly what you're getting – and there's very little difference in the taste of the finished pâté given that a relatively small quantity is used.

Now combine the onion and mixed vegetables in a large bowl and then add the brain, parsley, nutmeg, salt and pepper. Break 5 of the eggs into the bowl and mix them in slowly.

Heat the remaining oil and pour it into a high-sided soufflé dish (or cake mould, if you've got one) so that it completely covers the bottom. Transfer half the brain mixture into the soufflé dish, stir the remaining 5 eggs into the rest of the brain mixture and then add it to the soufflé dish.

Cook in an oven pre-heated to 180°C/350°F/gas mark 4 for 40 minutes, until the pâté is a light golden colour. You'll have to keep an eye on it, because if the pâté turns too dark that means it's becoming too dry.

Set aside to cool, slice and serve cold.

The sale of animal brains is now illegal in Britain, but, like the recipe for Brain in Paprika Sauce (p.74), this subtle pâté is typical of *pied noir* cooking and a delicious addition to any meal in countries where brains can still be bought.

A WORD ABOUT OLIVES

Olives are, of course, integral to North African cooking. Almost anywhere you look in the *souks* you can spot huge ceramic jars filled with olives of every possible size, colour and flavour, including olives seasoned with dried herbs, chillis or preserved lemons.

My mother would crush green olives on a hard surface with a heavy block of wood, always taking care not to split the pit, wash them, put them in a ceramic urn and fill it with water and salt. Over the course of the next two weeks she would change the water every day. On the fifteenth day she'd pour the contents of the urn – water and all – into glass jars to which she added slices of fresh lemon. She would start serving them the following day.

She bought her olive oil in the markets and occasionally spiked it with herbs or spices. By putting several sprigs of oregano into a jar of olive oil she created a delicious flavouring for salads. Alternatively, she would take four tablespoons of mild paprika, mix it into half a pint of olive oil and then put in a whole red chilli pepper. She would add this flavoured oil to the spices in her stuffed cabbage, *loubia*, shoulder of lamb or any fish dish. This oil with paprika gives a special taste and a beautiful reddish colour that is very typical of North Africa to any dish. Nowadays flavoured oils can be bought, normally at inflated prices, in delicatessens, but they are so easy to prepare at home that I can never understand why people buy them.

Olives show up in all Mediterranean cuisines, but they are salty and conventional wisdom has it that, before cooking with olives, you need to rinse them thoroughly in fresh water. We find that the best solution to this problem is simply dropping them in boiling water for five minutes before adding them to a dish; the saltiness is reduced without losing the distinctive flavour of olives.

Salads

THERE ARE NO RULES as to when salads should make their appearance in a *pied noir* meal. They can show up as part of the *kémia*, and often do so if the hostess feels she needs to fill up her table, or they can accompany the main course.

The matching of tastes and textures as contrast or counterfoil is, of course, very much a personal matter, and I find that either of the grilled pepper dishes or the cooked olive salad works best with couscous. If the main dish is grilled meat, such as a kebab, I usually serve a *salade pied noir*.

Generally speaking, we make two sorts of salads – fresh, which are mixtures of uncooked vegetables that are served cold, and cooked salads made with vegetables that have been prepared to be served either warm or cold.

We do, of course, also eat salads the way the French do, as an hors d'oeuvre, as a meal in itself – say a *salade Niçoise* – or as a big bowl of lettuce tossed with a vinaigrette at the end of a meal, but our salads belong more to the North African than the European tradition.

Salade Pied Noir

PIED NOIR SALAD

Preparation ✦ 30 minutes

4 tomatoes, diced
4 artichoke hearts, cut into quarters
Half a cucumber, peeled and thinly sliced
2 sticks of celery, cut into small pieces
10 radishes, lightly peeled and sliced
10 small cauliflower florets
2 red onions, thinly sliced
1 lemon, peeled and diced
3 hard-boiled eggs, shelled and sliced
150 g/5 oz olives (pitted or not, but use both
green and black)
2 tbsp balsamic vinegar
5 tbsp olive oil
1 tbsp lemon juice
A bunch of fresh basil, finely chopped
Salt
Pepper

This is our variation of *salade Niçoise*, but with the notable difference that we don't include tuna. We usually serve this salad as a first course, but it also shows up on our tables as a summer side dish to accompany *brochettes* and *kefta*.

Mix the vegetables and diced lemon together in a large bowl.

Mix the olive oil, balsamic vinegar, lemon juice, basil, salt and pepper in a smaller bowl, stir thoroughly and then pour over the vegetables.

Toss the salad and then decorate it with the olives and slices of hard-boiled egg.

Betteraves et Carottes au Cumin

BEETROOT AND CARROTS WITH CUMIN

Preparation ✦ 5 minutes
Cooking ✦ 30 minutes

500 g/1 lb beetroot
500 g/1 lb carrots
12 cloves of garlic
10 tbsp olive oil
6 tbsp wine vinegar
2 tsp mild paprika
2 tsp cumin
Salt
Pepper

Start with the beetroot. You can buy them pre-cooked, which is fine. If not, you'll have to boil them for 25 minutes, or until they're tender, and then remove their skin. Dice them and put them on one side of a large serving plate.

Trim the ends off the carrots, peel and wash them well, cut them into slices and cook them in boiling salted water for 15 minutes. Drain them and put them on the other half of the serving plate.

Now heat the olive oil in a frying pan, add the finely chopped garlic and mix in the cumin, paprika and salt and pepper. Finally, add the vinegar. Cook for 2 minutes, stirring frequently so that the spices don't burn, and then pour the sauce over the diced beetroot and sliced carrots.

Coeurs d'Artichauts à l'Orange et au Citron

ARTICHOKE HEARTS WITH ORANGE AND LEMON

Preparation ✦ 30 minutes
Cooking ✦ 45 minutes

12 artichoke hearts
2 oranges
2 lemons (1 to be juiced)
1 bay leaf
4 cloves of garlic
4 tbsp olive oil
½ tsp turmeric or a pinch of saffron
Salt
Pepper

After removing the leaves from the artichokes and cutting out the black, hairy choke, cut the hearts into 4 or 6 pieces.

Place them in a large bowl of cold water so that they are completely covered and stir in the juice of half a lemon. Allow to soak for 10 minutes. I find that artichokes always leave black stains on my hands; if you're not using gloves, the stains will wash off with lemon juice.

Meanwhile, fry the garlic in the oil, using a fairly high-sided saucepan. Pour a pint of fresh, cold water into the pan and add the rest of the lemon juice, the turmeric or saffron, bay leaf, salt and pepper. As soon as the water begins to boil, remove the artichoke hearts from the bowl in which they have been soaking, drop them into the pan and cook, uncovered, over a medium heat for 20 minutes.

Now peel and slice the oranges and the other lemon. Add the fruit to the saucepan and continue simmering for another 10 minutes. The water should by this time be considerably reduced, leaving only a thickish sauce.

Remove the bay leaf and serve the artichoke hearts on a plate, surrounded by the oranges and lemons and covered with the sauce.

This salad is traditionally served hot, but works very well served cold the next day.

Frita

GRILLED PEPPER AND TOMATO SALAD

Preparation ◆ 45 minutes
Cooking ◆ 30 minutes

6 red peppers
4 tomatoes
4 tbsp olive oil
3 cloves of garlic
1 small chilli
Salt
Pepper

Soak the tomatoes in boiling water for 2 minutes so that the skin is easily removed. Slice them in half, trim out the cores and seeds and cut them into small pieces.

Seed the chilli, and don't forget to wash your hands thoroughly afterwards. First grill the peppers and, when they're half-done, add the chilli, grilling them on all sides until their skins start to char. There are some people who insist that the next step is to place them in a plastic bag to cool, so that the skins can be easily removed, but there are others, like my mother, who claim that the peppers and chilli are best allowed to cool without being put into a bag and that the skin comes away just as easily if they're allowed to cool on a plate. In the end, I suspect, it's really just a question of habit. Now cut the seeds and stems out of the peppers and wash them under cold water.

Put the oil and the finely chopped garlic in a saucepan, add the tomato pieces and cook over a medium heat until the juices begin to reduce. Meanwhile, cut the peppers into small pieces and the chilli even more finely. When the tomatoes have cooked for 5 minutes, add the peppers and chilli. Season lightly with salt and pepper and simmer, covered, for another 10 minutes, stirring frequently.

My mother always brought this salad to the table hot, but I prefer to serve it cold as I find it lighter and fresher on the palate, so I always prepare it the night before.

Piments Grillés

GRILLED PEPPERS

Preparation ✦ 10 minutes
Cooking ✦ 20 minutes

*6 peppers (use several different colours,
mixing red, yellow and green)*
3 cloves of garlic
2 tbsp lemon juice
4 tbsp olive oil
Salt
Pepper

Grill, skin, seed and stem the peppers as in the previous recipe. Then cut them into nice long strips – you should be able to average 4 strips per pepper.

Lay the peppers in a serving dish, alternating the colours. Cover them with olive oil, lemon juice and the finely chopped garlic and add salt and pepper to taste.

My advice is to make these peppers a couple of hours in advance so that they can marinate in the sauce. They are delicious as a starter and, because they're so light, they work especially well before a heavy meal like couscous.

Poireaux Vinaigrette

LEEKS IN VINAIGRETTE

Preparation ◆ 20 minutes
Cooking ◆ 15 minutes

8 leeks, washed and trimmed
5 tbsp olive oil
2 tbsp balsamic vinegar
1 tsp Dijon mustard
4 cloves of garlic, finely chopped
A bunch of parsley, finely chopped
Salt
Pepper

This is a mainstream French dish that became a standard feature of *pied noir* cuisine because it is so perfectly suited the North African climate. I use balsamic vinegar in this recipe, which is, admittedly, an adaptation, as this delicately flavoured Italian vinegar was not available to us in North Africa 40 years ago – we used ordinary red wine vinegar. I am, however, absolutely convinced that, had balsamic vinegar been available, my grandmother would have been the first to use it.

The leeks are simply boiled in salted water, in a covered pan, for 10 minutes, then drained, cooled and arranged on a serving dish. Sprinkle with the parsley and garlic.

To make the sauce, vigorously mix the olive oil, balsamic vinegar, mustard, salt and pepper.

Serve slightly warm, doused in the vinaigrette.

Fèves Fraîches à la Vapeur et aux Olives Noires

SALAD OF STEAMED BROAD BEANS WITH BLACK OLIVES

Preparation ✦ 20 minutes
Cooking ✦ 15 minutes

2 kg / 4 lb fresh broad beans
200 g / 7 oz black olives
1 tsp cumin
Salt
Pepper

Shell the broad beans, then cook them in a steamer – we use the *couscoussier* – for 10-15 minutes, until they're tender. Put them in a dish, add the olives, which should not be pitted, salt, pepper and cumin. Serve with the beans still warm; alternatively, the salad can be eaten cold.

Frozen beans can be used when fresh broad beans aren't available – you will need just 4-5 minutes to cook them until they are tender.

Salade de Fenouil

FENNEL SALAD

Preparation ✦ 10 minutes
Cooking ✦ 40 minutes

4 fennel heads, cut into quarters
Juice of 1 lemon
4 tbsp olive oil
3 cloves of garlic, finely chopped
Salt

Fennel has a wonderful aniseed taste and we usually eat it raw, sprinkled with salt and pepper, but it can be cooked, and this is a fast, easy and delicious salad.

Heat the olive oil in a saucepan and fry the garlic until it is lightly browned. Then add half a pint of water and the lemon juice. As soon as it starts to boil, add the fennel and salt and cook, covered, over a high heat for 30 minutes.

When the sauce has reduced to about one-quarter of its original volume, it's ready.

Salade d'Olives Cuites

COOKED OLIVE SALAD

Preparation ✦ 30 minutes
Cooking ✦ 20 minutes

375 g / 12 oz green or violet olives, pitted
1 tomato, peeled and diced
4 cloves of garlic, finely chopped
3 tbsp olive oil

1 bay leaf
1 tsp mixed herbs (herbes de Provence)

Plunge the olives into boiling water for 3 minutes to reduce their saltiness and then drain them. Peel the tomato as in the recipe for *frita* (p.31).

Fry the garlic in olive oil in a saucepan over a medium heat. After 5 minutes add the tomato, bay leaf, herbs, olives and enough water to cover all the ingredients. Now cover the saucepan and, still over a medium heat, cook for 15 minutes, until the sauce is reduced. Serve either hot or cold.

Salade de Pois Chiches au Paprika et au Cumin

CHICK-PEA SALAD WITH PAPRIKA AND CUMIN

Preparation ✦ 10 minutes
Cooking ✦ 10 minutes

375 g/12 oz (1 tin) chick-peas
6 cloves of garlic, finely chopped
2 tbsp cumin
1 tsp mild paprika
3 tbsp olive oil
1 tbsp red wine vinegar
1 tsp salt

We always used to make this dish with dried chick-peas, which caused a lot of extra trouble as the chick-peas needed to be soaked overnight and then boiled for at least 40 minutes before they could be cooked with the rest of the ingredients. This was a great deal of work and also, of course, involved a degree of planning, for what is, otherwise, a very simple salad. Anyway, tinned chick-peas taste just as good as the freshly soaked and cooked variety.

Fry the garlic in oil, then add the cumin, paprika, salt and vinegar. Cook for 3 minutes, stirring frequently so that the spices don't burn, and then add the drained chick-peas. Stir thoroughly so that all the chick-peas are covered with the sauce and fry for a further 5 minutes, still stirring regularly.

Caviar d'Aubergines avec Mayonnaise Maison

AUBERGINE CAVIARE WITH HOME-MADE MAYONNAISE

Preparation ✦ 45 minutes
Cooking ✦ 30 minutes

3 medium-sized aubergines
2 hard-boiled eggs
1 clove of garlic
Juice of half a lemon
Salt
Pepper

For the mayonnaise
1 egg-yolk
1 tsp Dijon mustard
8 tbsp vegetable oil
Juice of half a lemon
Salt
Pepper

This is a cold dish that works as an entrée and equally well as a side dish. There are all sorts of variations to it throughout the Arab world and the Middle East – some use olive oil instead of mayonnaise, others add garlic and cumin – but this is the recipe my mother used.

Begin by grilling the aubergines the same way you do for the grilled peppers (p.31), until the skin blackens. Pushing a skewer lengthways through the aubergines makes turning them easier. Peel the aubergines while still warm and pull off their stems. Then put them in a colander under a heavy plate to drain off the bitter juices and set aside.

While the aubergines are cooling, make the mayonnaise in a small bowl by combining the egg-yolk, mustard, oil, salt and pepper, and mixing slowly with a fork.

My grandmother had two tricks when it came to making mayonnaise. Firstly, she always used older eggs. In other words, if you've got some eggs that have been in the fridge for a few days, choose one of them rather than a fresher egg. Secondly, she was always particularly slow when it came to adding oil. One drop too many or, for that matter, one drop too fast and the mayonnaise is ruined. The advantage of making mayonnaise at home is the taste. It is quite different from anything you buy in a jar, and once you've tasted the difference it's very hard to think of ever using the bought variety.

That done, blend the aubergines with the peeled garlic and the hard-boiled eggs until you have a purée. Transfer the mixture to a bowl with the mayonnaise, lemon juice, salt and pepper and stir well with a wooden spoon. Serve cold.

Pruneaux aux Noix

PRUNES STUFFED WITH WALNUTS

Preparation ✦ 15 minutes
Cooking ✦ 20 minutes

250 g/8 oz shelled walnuts
500 g/1 lb pitted prunes
4 tbsp castor sugar
2 oranges
3 tbsp vegetable oil

Stuff a walnut into each of the prunes and lay them carefully in a saucepan with the oil. Now squeeze both oranges and add their juice and the sugar to the prunes.

Put the saucepan over a very low heat and cook the prunes for 20 minutes, basting them with the juice from the pan every few minutes.

Use the prunes and walnuts to accompany meat or chicken. I know people who serve *pruneaux aux noix* sprinkled with cinnamon, and anyone who likes cinnamon will love them presented this way, but deep down I can't help but think that this is gilding the lily.

Salade de Pommes de Terre

POTATO SALAD

Preparation ✦ 30 minutes
Cooking ✦ 30 minutes

6 medium-sized potatoes
6 tbsp olive oil

2 tbsp wine vinegar or balsamic vinegar
3 small shallots
2 tbsp parsley, finely chopped
Salt
Pepper

No one would ever dream of claiming that this is a specifically *pied noir* recipe, but *salade de pommes de terre* features so
frequently in our meals that no collection of the recipes
which we enjoyed in North Africa would be complete
without it.

Boil the potatoes in salted water for about 30 minutes or
until they're just done. While the potatoes are cooking, slice
the shallots very finely and add them to a vinaigrette made
with the oil, vinegar, half of the parsley and salt and pepper.

When the potatoes are cooked, drain and peel them as
soon as you're able to handle them. Then dice the potatoes
and, while they're still warm, mix them with the dressing.
Sprinkle the rest of the parsley over the potatoes and serve
either warm or chilled.

Salade de pommes de terre goes particularly well with *kefta*
(p.65) or *kebabs* (p.69).

Oeufs Mimosa avec Mayonnaise Maison

MIMOSA EGGS WITH HOME-MADE MAYONNAISE

Preparation ✦ 10 minutes
Cooking ✦ 10 minutes

6 eggs
Home-made mayonnaise (see p.37)

This is the simplest recipe in this book, yet it is also one of the most attractive appetisers and never fails to please.

Boil the eggs for 8 to 10 minutes. Run them under cold water while taking off the shells and then cut them in half. Take 10 of the 12 egg halves, place a tablespoon of mayonnaise on each and lay them on a plate. Now, using a cheese grater, take the remaining egg and sprinkle the gratings on top of the mayonnaise which covers the halved hard-boiled eggs.

Salade d'Aubergine avec Poivron Rouge et Citron

AUBERGINE SALAD WITH RED PEPPER AND LEMON

Preparation ✦ 30 minutes
Cooking ✦ 25 minutes

1 large or 2 small aubergines
1 red pepper
1 lemon, preferably unwaxed
3 tbsp vegetable oil
3 cloves of garlic
1 tsp mild paprika
1 tsp cumin
Salt
Pepper

First of all, dice the aubergine, sprinkle it with salt and leave it to drain in a colander for about 20 minutes. Then dice the whole lemon, including the peel, remove the pips and salt it in the same way as the aubergine, also leaving it for 20 minutes.

Remove the core and seeds from the pepper, rinse it well under running water and dice it. Now gently squeeze out any excess moisture from the aubergine and pat it dry with kitchen paper.

Fry the chopped garlic in oil over a medium heat and, when it is lightly browned, add the aubergines, lemon and pepper. Cook them together for 20 minutes, constantly stirring the mixture. Five minutes before the end of the cooking time check the flavour and add the paprika, cumin, pepper and, if needed, a little more salt. Served warm or cold, this salad is a delicious accompaniment to *poulet aux olives* (p.79) or *poulet aux pruneaux et aux amandes* (p.100).

Concombres à la Menthe

CUCUMBER AND MINT SALAD

Preparation ✦ 15 minutes

2 medium-sized cucumbers
A bunch of mint, finely chopped
5 tbsp olive oil
1 tbsp lemon juice
Salt
Pepper

This is a very simple, refreshing appetiser which makes a perfect start to a summer meal.

First of all, peel and trim the cucumbers, and then slice them very thinly. Make the dressing by mixing the lemon juice, olive oil, salt and pepper in a bowl, and then stir in the cucumber slices.

Chill the dressed cucumber for 15 minutes and then add the finely chopped mint just before serving.

Vegetables

WE WERE VERY FORTUNATE in Casablanca because all the vegetables we wanted – tomatoes, aubergines, peppers, artichokes, courgettes, beans, onions, leeks, garlic, fennel, radishes, carrots – were grown nearby and arrived fresh in the *souks* every morning. This ready availability of a wide variety of fresh vegetables formed one of the cornerstones of our cuisine and *pied noir* cooks are still very particular about the freshness and quality of their vegetables.

Stuffed vegetables often make an appearance at our meals. When stuffing vegetables, my mother always bought a good piece of steak and minced it herself by hand, and my sister in Marseilles still prepares it that way, although I find I can rely on my butcher to grind it for me. The trick is in using the highest quality beef rather than relying on the pre-minced, pre-packaged supermarket variety.

Stuffed vegetables appear in many different cuisines, of

course, and my husband assures me that his grandmothers, whose own mothers came from Hungary and Germany, made the best stuffed cabbage on earth, but theirs was a slightly sweet dish which included rice and raisins in the stuffing. The *pied noir* version, which relies on different flavourings, is rather more savoury.

Chou Farci

STUFFED CABBAGE

Preparation ✦ 40 minutes
Cooking ✦ 1 hour 10 minutes

500 g/1 lb minced beef
2 tbsp short-grain rice
2 cloves of garlic
A bunch of parsley, finely chopped
A pinch of nutmeg
2 eggs
1 large green cabbage
1 onion
500 g/1 lb tomatoes, diced
2 tbsp vegetable oil
Salt
Pepper

Mix the meat with the rice, garlic, parsley, nutmeg, salt, pepper and, finally, the eggs in a large bowl, roll the mixture into small balls and put to one side.

Separate the cabbage leaves and boil them in salted water for 10 minutes. When they're done, remove the leaves and allow them to dry on a kitchen towel.

Then, taking one leaf at a time, add a meatball and wrap it up like a small packet. If the cabbage leaves won't stay closed on their own, you can hold them shut with a toothpick.

Fry the tomatoes and onion over a medium heat in a large frying pan, pour in a glass of water, stir constantly and, after 5 minutes, add the stuffed cabbage leaves. Cook for 20 minutes and then reduce the heat, cover and cook for a further 30 minutes, topping up the water if necessary.

This dish goes particularly well with basmati rice.

Aubergines Farcies

STUFFED AUBERGINES

Preparation ✦ 40 minutes
Cooking ✦ 1 hour 15 minutes

4 aubergines
2 onions, chopped
2 cloves of garlic
1 tsp nutmeg
A small bunch of parsley, finely chopped
2 eggs
A handful of white bread with the crust removed
375 g / 12 oz minced beef
8 tbsp vegetable oil
50 g / 2 oz semolina or breadcrumbs
1 tomato, diced
1 bay leaf
1 tsp turmeric
Salt
Pepper
3 potatoes, cut into quarters (optional)

Begin by peeling the aubergines, cutting them in half lengthways and scooping out their insides. Discard the flesh – the idea is to leave a good-sized shell. Salt the shells and set them aside for 15 minutes. Then soak the bread in water.

To prepare the stuffing, take the freshly minced beef, add one of the onions, the finely chopped garlic, parsley, the bread (which should have any surplus water squeezed out), nutmeg, salt, pepper and one of the eggs. Mix all the ingredients together by hand.

Put the semolina or breadcrumbs – you can use either, although I prefer semolina – on a plate; this is to be used to coat the aubergines. Beat the second egg in a bowl.

Now wash the aubergine shells, dry them and fill them with the minced beef mixture. Once that's done, roll each aubergine shell in the egg and then in the semolina or breadcrumbs.

Pour half the oil into a frying pan and fry the stuffed aubergines on both sides, but only until the meat becomes light brown.

Then, using the rest of the oil, begin to fry the second onion in a heavy saucepan. Add the tomato, turmeric, bay leaf and, finally, a pint of water. Then add the stuffed aubergines and cook them for 1 hour, during which time the sauce will thicken. Add salt and pepper to taste.

To make this dish a little heartier, you can add 3 potatoes to the sauce 15 minutes before the end of the cooking time.

Artichauts Farcis

STUFFED ARTICHOKES

Preparation ✦ 40 minutes
Cooking ✦ 1 hour 20 minutes

6 artichokes
Juice of half a lemon
350 g / 12 oz minced beef
½ tsp nutmeg
A small bunch of parsley, finely chopped
A handful of white bread with the crust removed
2 eggs
6 tbsp vegetable oil
2 onions, chopped
1 tomato, skinned and diced
1 tsp turmeric
1 bay leaf
500 g / 1 lb green beans, trimmed
500 g / 1 lb potatoes, cut into quarters
50 g / 2 oz semolina or breadcrumbs
Salt
Pepper

Remove the leaves and the small black hairs from the artichokes, leaving the hearts, and soak these in a bowl of water with the juice of half a lemon. At the same time soak the bread in water.

Mix the minced beef with one of the onions, nutmeg, parsley, white bread (which should have any surplus water squeezed out), salt, pepper and one of the eggs. Make six small balls and stuff them into the depression in the artichoke hearts.

Break the other egg in a bowl and put the semolina or

breadcrumbs into another. Roll the meat side of the stuffed artichoke first in the egg and then in the semolina or bread-crumbs.

Heat 2 tablespoons of the oil in a saucepan and fry the stuffed artichokes until the meat turns light brown.

When this is done, heat the remaining oil in a heavy saucepan over a medium heat and add the second onion and the tomato. After 5 minutes add 2 pints of water, the turmeric and the bay leaf. Reduce the heat, add the arti-chokes and salt and pepper to the cooking liquid. Cover and cook for 30 minutes. At this point add the green beans and the potatoes and cook, still covered, for another half-hour, allowing the juices to thicken.

This stuffing works equally well with courgettes, peppers or tomatoes.

La Tchouchouka

PIED NOIR RATATOUILLE

Preparation ✦ 30 minutes
Cooking ✦ 40 minutes

2 red peppers
2 green peppers
2 medium-sized aubergines
3 courgettes
2 onions
4 medium-sized tomatoes
6 cloves of garlic
A small bunch of parsley
1 bay leaf
1 tsp thyme
A bunch of basil

6 tbsp olive oil
Salt
Pepper

First of all, dice the aubergines, sprinkle them with salt and leave them to drain in a colander for 20 minutes or so; then rinse off the salt and dry them. Meanwhile, wash, stem, seed, peel and dice the other vegetables.

Put the olive oil, garlic, bay leaf, basil, thyme and parsley in a large saucepan and fry the vegetables over a medium heat. Start with the aubergines, then add the peppers, onions, tomatoes and, finally, the courgettes. Reduce the heat, add salt and pepper and stir occasionally, until the tomatoes attain the consistency of a purée. Cover the pan and cook for 25 minutes, by when the vegetables should be very tender.

Like *ratatouille*, this dish can be eaten cold or warm, as an appetiser, a main dish or with meat.

Brania

AUBERGINES AND CHICK-PEAS WITH BEEF

Preparation ✦ 40 minutes
Cooking ✦ 1 hour 30 minutes

2 aubergines
750 g / 1½ lb diced fillet of beef
400 g / 14 oz chick-peas, soaked overnight
1 clove of garlic
4 tbsp vegetable oil
1 tsp cumin
1 tsp mild paprika
Salt

Cut the aubergines into 1 inch slices, sprinkle them with salt and leave to drain in a colander for 20–30 minutes, thus allowing the salt to draw out the aubergine's bitter juices.

Put the chick-peas, meat and garlic in a heavy saucepan, cover with water and cook, covered, over a medium heat for 30 minutes.

Rinse and dry the aubergines. Then heat the oil in a large frying pan and cook the aubergines until they're soft – this should take around 10 minutes. As soon as they're done, drain them and dry them on kitchen paper.

When the chick-peas have cooked for 30 minutes, add the aubergines, the cumin and the paprika, reduce the heat slightly and cook, still covered, for another half-hour, by when the sauce will have thickened.

Pâté de Pommes de Terre

POTATO CAKES

Preparation ✦ 20 minutes
Cooking ✦ 30 minutes

6 large potatoes
5 tbsp vegetable oil
2 eggs
125 g / 4 oz breadcrumbs or matzo meal
1 tsp nutmeg
Salt
Pepper

Peel the potatoes, then boil them in salted water until cooked, for around 15–20 minutes depending on the size of the potatoes. Mash them while they're still hot, add a table-spoon of the oil, the nutmeg, one of the eggs, salt and pepper and shape them into patties about 3 inches in diameter. (It is important that you mash the potatoes by hand – if a food-processor is used the potato will be too runny to form into potato cakes.)

Beat the second egg, roll the potato cakes in it and then in the breadcrumbs or matzo meal. Now heat the remaining oil in a large frying pan and cook the potato cakes for about 5 minutes on each side until they're a beautiful golden colour. Serve hot.

The version made with matzo meal is often served during Passover.

Courgettes Sauce Mousseline

COURGETTES IN MOUSSELINE SAUCE

Preparation ✦ 15 minutes
Cooking ✦ 20 minutes

8-10 courgettes
1 egg
5 tbsp vegetable oil
2 tsp lemon juice
1 tsp Dijon mustard
Salt
Pepper

Trim the ends off the courgettes and then peel them verti-cally so as to remove the skin in alternate strips. In other words, peel one strip and skip the next, leaving the skin in place. Repeat so that you remove half of the skin. Then boil the courgettes for 10-12 minutes, making sure that they don't become mushy – they should be *al dente*. When they're done, slice the courgettes and lay them out on a plate.

Now make a mayonnaise. Take the yolk of the egg and add Dijon mustard, salt and pepper. While stirring the mixture with a fork, pour in the oil very slowly. This should take about 5 minutes. Then beat the egg-white and add it and the lemon juice to the mayonnaise.

Pour the sauce over the courgettes and serve.

This sauce also makes a good accompaniment for asparagus.

Soufflé aux Courgettes

COURGETTE SOUFFLÉ

Preparation ✦ 30 minutes
Cooking ✦ 50 minutes

6 medium-sized courgettes
2 onions
3 cloves of garlic
3-4 tbsp olive oil
6 eggs
200 g / 7 oz Emmental, grated
Salt
Pepper

Trim and scrape the courgettes before cutting them into slices about ¼ inch thick. Then sweat the finely chopped onions and garlic in a large saucepan until they are translucent, add the courgettes and cook, uncovered, until tender, which should take 15 to 20 minutes. Stir occasionally and, when the courgettes are done, allow them to cool.

Beat the eggs in a large bowl and add the grated cheese, mixing well until the Emmental and the eggs are thoroughly combined. Then add the courgette mixture, salt and pepper and continue to stir the ingredients with a wooden spoon, but do so with a light hand so as not to break up the tender courgette slices.

Pre-heat the oven to 170°C/325°F/gas mark 3. Transfer the mixture to an oven-proof dish and bake for 30 minutes until it turns a beautiful golden colour.

This soufflé makes a particularly good accompaniment for fish.

There is a simple variation on this recipe which uses spinach instead of courgettes – just defrost 1 pound of frozen spinach and substitute it for the courgettes.

Soups

BECAUSE WE LIVED in a warm climate, we are not soup-eaters in the same way that the French and other Europeans are. When we lived in Casablanca, soup was usually reserved for chilly winter nights, when it was often served as a meal in its own right. Perhaps most typical is *harira*, the best known Moroccan soup, which we adapted from the Arabs. It is a dish which they make to break their fast during Ramadan.

Harira

CHICKEN, LAMB AND VEGETABLE SOUP

Preparation ✦ 20 minutes
Cooking ✦ 2 hours

8 chicken wings
1 set chicken giblets
1 chicken neck
500g/1lb lamb, cut into small cubes
1 onion, finely chopped
150g/5oz chick-peas, soaked overnight
150g/5oz brown lentils, soaked overnight
3 tomatoes, skinned and chopped
150g/5oz fine soup noodles
2 sticks of celery, finely chopped
50g/2oz butter
1/2 tsp cinnamon
2 tbsp fresh coriander, chopped
2 tbsp fresh parsley, chopped
1 tsp turmeric
1 tsp saffron
1 tsp ginger
Juice of half a lemon and 1 tsp dried yeast
– or –
2 tbsp flour
– or –
2 egg-yolks
Salt
Pepper

Place the butter, chicken, lamb, onion, tomatoes and 4 pints of water in a very large saucepan, bring to the boil and cook over a medium heat, skimming the surface regularly.

After 30 minutes add the cinnamon, saffron, parsley, chick-peas, lentils and celery.

An hour later lower the heat and add the noodles, coriander, salt, pepper, turmeric and ginger. Cover and simmer for a further half-hour.

About 10 minutes before serving, you'll need to thicken the broth. There are several ways of doing this. Some people dilute yeast with water and lemon juice and add it to the soup. Others, using a more traditional French method, thicken their soup with 2 tablespoons of flour. I simply stir in 2 beaten egg-yolks, making sure that the soup is off the boil when they're added, otherwise you end up with strings of cooked egg, which don't look very attractive and don't thicken the soup.

Soupe à l'Ail

GARLIC SOUP

Preparation ✦ 5 minutes
Cooking ✦ 15 minutes

6 cloves of garlic, finely chopped
100 g / 4 oz fine vermicelli
1 tbsp olive oil
50 g / 2 oz butter
2 egg-yolks
50 g / 2 oz Gruyère, grated
Salt
Pepper

This easily made, healthy and tasty garlic soup always reminds me of my mother's kitchen.

Brown the garlic slowly in oil in a saucepan. Add 1 pint

of cold water and some salt, bring to the boil and stir in the vermicelli.

Meanwhile, melt the butter, pour it into a bowl and mix it with the egg-yolks. When the garlic and vermicelli have boiled for between 5 and 10 minutes, add the butter and egg-yolks, taking care that the soup is off the boil.

Finally, stir in the grated cheese, add plenty of freshly ground black pepper and serve immediately.

Boketof

VEGETABLE SOUP WITH BEEF

Preparation ✦ 30 minutes for the pasta, 30 minutes for the soup
Cooking ✦ 2 hours 30 minutes

For the soup
500 g / 1 lb shin of beef
200 g / 7 oz dried broad beans, soaked overnight
2 onions, finely chopped
2 tomatoes, peeled and diced
200 g / 7 oz courgettes, chopped
4 tbsp vegetable oil
1 tsp mild paprika
A small bunch of fresh coriander, chopped
200 g / 7 oz home-made or bought fresh pasta (see below)
Salt
Pepper

For the pasta
200 g / 7 oz plain flour
60 g / 2 oz yeast, fresh or dried
Warm water

My mother still prepares her own fresh pasta for *boketof.* The night before making the soup she combines the flour, yeast and water in a large bowl and then transfers it to a working surface where she kneads the dough until the mixture is smooth and elastic. Once that's done, she puts it back in a bowl which she covers with a tea-towel and allows the dough to rise for two hours.

When it has doubled in size, she takes a tray covered with a clean tea-towel and starts to shape the pasta, making spaghetti-like strands about 2 inches long but roughly three times thicker than ordinary spaghetti. She lays them out one by one on the tray, then covers them again with another tea-towel and leaves them overnight. The following morning the pasta strands are dry enough to put them in the soup.

Nowadays, of course, few of us find the time to make fresh pasta and most people buy it ready-made.

To make the soup she heats the oil in a large, heavy pan over a medium heat and fries the meat. To that she adds the onions, tomatoes, drained broad beans, paprika and about 4 pints of water. After 30 minutes she reduces the heat and allows the dish to cook gently for 2 hours.

10 minutes before the end of the cooking she seasons the soup with salt and pepper and then adds the pasta and the courgettes. Make sure there is enough liquid in the pan because, after all, this is a soup. If you need more water, always add cold water.

She adds the coriander immediately before serving.

To make the soup that little bit more special, she always puts a small dish of *harissa* (p.116) on the table for those of us who like a dash of chilli.

Soupe de Bessara

BROAD BEAN SOUP

Preparation ✦ 10 minutes
Cooking ✦ 1 hour

250 g / 8 oz dried broad beans, soaked overnight
6 cloves of garlic
Juice of 1 lemon
3 tbsp olive oil
1 tbsp vegetable oil
1 tsp cumin
1 tsp chilli powder (hot or mild, depending on your taste)
Salt
Pepper

Bring 4 pints of water to the boil in a large saucepan. Drain the beans and add them to the boiling water, followed by the vegetable oil. Then chop the garlic, mix it with the cumin and add to the soup. Reduce the heat and cook for 50 minutes, until the beans are very soft. Add a little more water if you need to.

Blend the soup in a food-processor to obtain a very soft purée. Return it to the saucepan, add the salt, lemon juice, chilli powder, another pinch of cumin, salt and pepper and cook for 4 to 5 minutes. Then add the olive oil and cook for a further 3 minutes, stirring constantly with a wooden spoon to improve the soup's consistency.

Remove from the heat and serve immediately because the soup will stiffen as it cools.

Soupe de Poulet

CHICKEN SOUP

Preparation ✦ 20 minutes
Cooking ✦ 1 hour 30 minutes

1 chicken
2 carrots, peeled and chopped
1 tomato, skinned and diced
2 onions, finely chopped
1 leek, chopped
2 sticks of celery, chopped
125 g / 4 oz vermicelli
1 bay leaf
½ tsp thyme
A small bunch of parsley
2 tbsp olive oil
Salt
Pepper

Put the olive oil, vegetables, herbs, salt and pepper in a large pot over a medium heat and stir constantly for 5 minutes. Now add the whole chicken, which should be thoroughly cleaned and rinsed, to the vegetables. Add 4 pints of water, reduce the heat, cover and cook for 1 hour.

About a quarter of an hour before serving add the vermicelli. At this point you might also need to add a little more water – there should be enough to cover the chicken.

To serve, cut up the chicken, put the pieces into a tureen, add the chopped parsley and pour the soup over the meat.

Soupe à la Menthe Fraîche

FRESH MINT SOUP

Preparation ✦ 15 minutes
Cooking ✦ 1 hour, not including the chicken stock

2 ½ litres / 5 pints chicken stock
2 onions, finely chopped
3 potatoes, cubed
3 courgettes, chopped
2 tomatoes, skinned and chopped
3 tbsp vegetable oil
20 mint leaves
10 basil leaves
150 g / 5 oz vermicelli
Juice of half a lemon
Salt
Pepper

Fry the onions in the oil for 3 minutes, then add the tomatoes, potatoes and courgettes, lower the heat and allow to simmer for 15 minutes. Take care to keep the heat low enough that the mixture doesn't stick to the bottom of the pan and burn.

Salt and pepper the mixture before adding the chicken stock. Stir in the stock, add the vermicelli and cook for half an hour. Three minutes before the end of the cooking add the finely chopped mint and basil leaves and then, just before you're ready to take it off the stove, add the lemon juice.

Soupe à l'Orge Perlé

BARLEY SOUP

Preparation ✦ 15 minutes
Cooking ✦ 1 hour

250 g/8 oz barley
1 large onion, finely chopped
1 marrow bone
3 tbsp tomato purée
2 tbsp vegetable oil
A small bunch of coriander
Salt
Pepper
375 g/12 oz shin of beef (optional)

First, wash the barley thoroughly. Then heat the oil in a large saucepan and, after browning the onion, add the tomato purée, barley, marrow bone, salt and pepper. Cover the ingredients with water and cook gently, covered, for 1 hour.

To make even more of a meal of this soup, you can add shin of beef at the same time that you add the marrow bone. Sprinkle with chopped coriander before serving.

Potage aux Navets et Fèves

TURNIP AND DRIED BEAN SOUP

Preparation ✦ 30 minutes
Cooking ✦ 2 hours

500 g/1 lb shin of beef, cut into 3-4 pieces
2 onions, finely chopped

150 g / 5 oz dried fava beans
400 g / 14 oz young turnips, peeled and quartered
1 tomato, peeled and diced
2 tbsp vegetable oil
A stick of celery, chopped
1 tsp mild paprika
1 bay leaf
Salt
Pepper

Heat the oil over a medium heat in a large saucepan, add the turnips, onions, tomato, celery, fava beans – which need not be soaked in advance – and the bay leaf and brown them lightly. Then add 4 pints of water. Cover and cook for 1 hour.

Add the meat and continue to cook gently for another hour.

When that's ready, discard the bay leaf and put the meat to one side. Now, purée the vegetables in a food-processor, return the mixture to the saucepan to keep it hot and season with salt, pepper and paprika.

Finally, place the meat in a tureen and pour the soup over it. Mustard is not normally served with soups, but Dijon mustard goes well with this dish, as it does with a *pot-au-feu*.

Meat

LAMB, BEEF AND VEAL are the meats which feature most frequently in our cooking. We use all cuts and make much more use of offal, and particularly calf's brain, tongue, tripe and liver, than many other cuisines. One of our tastiest dishes is called *rate farcie*, which is spleen stuffed with minced beef and chicken livers and seasoned with cumin, paprika, coriander and black pepper. But spleen, like other types of offal, is not particularly fashionable nowadays – indeed, it's not easy to find even in France – and because it isn't necessarily to everyone's taste I haven't included it here. You're most likely to find it as street food in Morocco and, these days, even in some of the larger towns in the South of France – I last saw it at a stand near the port in Marseilles.

I have not included any recipes involving pork. This is not a meat we generally use, nor is it one that is easily found in the Muslim world. Pork products like *saucisson* were available to us when the French ruled North Africa, but Arabs, like Jews who keep kosher, don't eat pork and the Arab-Jewish influence is, of course, fundamental to this cuisine.

Kefta

GRILLED MINCED MEAT

Preparation ✦ 10 minutes
Cooking ✦ 5-10 minutes

500 g / 1 lb minced beef
2 cloves of garlic, finely chopped
1 tsp cumin
1 tsp mild paprika
1/2 tsp powdered coriander
Salt
Pepper

Mix the minced beef, which should not be too lean, with the garlic, cumin, paprika, coriander, salt and pepper. Form into small burgers and, if possible, grill them over charcoal.

The Arabs make their *kefta* with lamb and you can buy them at stalls in the *souks*. Grilled meats – *kefta* and *kebabs* – lend a lovely aroma to the markets in Morocco. The *kefta* in cities like Casablanca and Marrakech, Tangiers and Fez, are very good, but our mother never liked us eating street food, and anyway she always made her *kefta* with beef rather than lamb and served them to us with roast potatoes.

T'fina de Boeuf

BEEF WITH CHICK-PEAS

Preparation ✦ 30 minutes
Cooking ✦ 5 hours

375 g/12 oz chick-peas, soaked overnight
750 g/1½ lb shin of beef
1 marrow bone
6-8 small potatoes
4 eggs
1 tbsp vegetable oil
1 bulb of garlic
1 tsp mild paprika
Salt
Pepper

T'fina is a dish that used to appear for Saturday lunch having cooked slowly all night. Some families made their *t'fina* on a *plata,* a type of electric hotplate which was found in all *pied noir* households, but many religious Jews in Morocco would not use electricity after sunset on Friday so their *t'fina* had to be prepared before the Sabbath. Their maids would then take the *t'fina* in a casserole to the local bakery where it would be cooked overnight in the bread oven. The baker would mark a number on each pot with a red crayon and then give the maid a piece of paper with the same number on it. The next morning she'd return to the bakery with the slip of paper to pick up the *t'fina.*

Every bakery cooked *t'fina* in exactly the same way, yet each of my aunts would swear that her baker was better than any other because her *t'fina* came out with precisely the right consistency, which meant something like a good thick jam.

I've used chick-peas and beef here, because this is the way my mother usually makes *t'fina*. Every now and then, however, she changes the recipe and uses white kidney beans or fava beans. I sometimes ring the changes by using sweet potatoes, but my mother always uses plain whites. Sometimes she also includes a calf's foot in this dish, which she asks her butcher to chop into thirds. She simply throws it into the pot for added flavour, but this isn't strictly necessary.

Place the meat in the middle of a large pan and surround it with the drained chick-peas, the whole peeled potatoes, the peeled but unchopped garlic and the marrow bone. Then carefully lay the eggs, still in their shells, on top of the other ingredients. Now add the paprika, salt, pepper, oil and, finally, 4 pints of water.

Simmer over a very low heat for 4 hours, never allowing the water to boil. If you need to top it up so that the meat doesn't stick or burn, add a glass of cold water half-way through. But this is not a soup and the juices should reduce considerably by the time the dish is cooked.

To serve, put the meat in the middle of a large dish. The chick-peas and potatoes go around the meat and the eggs, now peeled and sliced, form an attractive outer ring.

After this filling dish we never had a dessert – instead, everyone took a siesta! Later my parents, uncles and aunts always played a Spanish card game called *la ronda* and we would all have tea and pastries, and I always associate *t'fina de boeuf* with that particular card game.

Langue aux Olives et aux Champignons

TONGUE WITH OLIVES AND MUSHROOMS

Preparation ✦ 30 minutes
Cooking ✦ 3 hours

1 tongue (ox or calf's)
4 cloves
250 g / 8 oz green olives, pitted
1 small glass white wine
3 tbsp vegetable oil
1 onion
2 tomatoes, diced
4 cloves of garlic
A bunch of parsley
300 g / 10 oz sliced mushrooms
Salt
Pepper

Pin the cloves into the tongue and boil it in salted water for an hour. While this is cooking, blanche the olives in boiling water for a couple of minutes or the dish runs the risk of being too salty. When the tongue is done, drain it and allow it to cool sufficiently so that you can remove the skin and then rinse it. Now place it in a pan with the oil, onions, garlic, tomatoes, salt and pepper. Pour in the wine and cook, covered, over a medium heat for another hour.

Then remove the tongue from the pan, allow it to cool once again and cut it into slices about half an inch thick. Return it to the pan and add the olives and mushrooms and a little more water if needed. Reduce the heat and simmer, still covered, for a third and final hour.

Add the chopped parsley just before serving.

Kebab

LAMB, LIVER AND BEEF BROCHETTES

Preparation ✦ 20 minutes
Cooking ✦ 5-10 minutes

500 g/1 lb lamb or mutton, cut into cubes
500 g/1 lb fillet of beef, cut into cubes
500 g/1 lb lamb's or calf's liver, cut into cubes
1 tbsp cumin
1 tbsp mild paprika
Salt
Pepper

This is one of the best known North African and Middle Eastern dishes. We put several different kinds of meat on skewers, but our kebabs differ from the Turkish variety in not interspersing onions or other vegetables between the meat.

We simply put between 6 and 8 alternating cubes of meat on a skewer, season and barbecue them. They can be cooked inside, under the grill, but they tend to make a lot of smoke and kebabs are much better cooked outside over charcoal. My mother always buys some pieces of fat which she adds to the skewers, alternating them with the meat, but I find that kebabs work just as well if I ask my butcher not to cut the beef too lean.

One of the attractions of kebabs is that they are very flexible – they can be eaten with pitta bread seasoned with a little *harissa* (p.116), with rice or with a salad.

Boulettes de Viande au Citron

MEATBALLS WITH LEMON

Preparation ✦ 20 minutes
Cooking ✦ 45 minutes

500 g/1 lb minced steak
50 g/2 oz white bread
2 lemons – 1 peeled and sliced, 1 juiced
2 eggs
1 onion
2 potatoes, cut into quarters
2 cloves of garlic, chopped
5 tbsp vegetable oil
A small bunch of parsley
A pinch of nutmeg
Salt
Pepper

Remove the crust from the bread, soak it in water and then squeeze out any surplus liquid. Mix the meat with the bread, chopped onion, nutmeg, salt and pepper in a large bowl and then add the finely chopped parsley and beaten eggs. Roll the mixture into small balls and put to one side.

Heat the oil in a saucepan, fry the garlic until it turns translucent, add half a pint of water, the potatoes, lemon juice, slices of lemon and, finally, the meatballs.

Cook, covered, over a medium heat for 30 minutes.

Boulettes de Viande aux Petits Pois

MEATBALLS WITH GREEN PEAS

Preparation ✦ 30 minutes
Cooking ✦ 45 minutes

For the meatballs
500 g/1 lb minced beef
2 cloves of garlic
A handful of white bread
50 g/2 oz breadcrumbs or semolina
A small bunch of parsley
1 tsp nutmeg
3 eggs
3 tbsp vegetable oil
Salt
Pepper

For the sauce
500 g/1 lb frozen peas
1 onion, chopped
2 tomatoes, skinned and chopped
2 medium-sized potatoes, cut into quarters
1 tsp turmeric
1 bay leaf
3 tbsp vegetable oil
Salt
Pepper

This is a simple but very tasty dish that often makes an appearance on *pied noir* tables on Friday nights if chicken or couscous isn't on the menu. It is a particular favourite of my children.

Soak the bread in water and squeeze out any surplus liquid. Mix together the meat, the finely chopped garlic, the wet bread, the finely chopped parsley, the nutmeg, salt and pepper and, finally, 2 of the eggs. Thoroughly mix all the ingredients together in a big bowl and then form the mixture into small balls.

Beat the remaining egg and, one by one, roll each meatball in it. Pour the breadcrumbs or semolina onto a plate and roll the meatballs in them. Heat the oil in a frying pan, add the meatballs and fry them for 10 minutes, after which they should be golden brown.

Now, using a large saucepan, fry the onion until it's soft, add the bay leaf and chopped tomatoes and cook for 3-5 minutes. Then add 3 glasses of water and the still frozen peas, the potatoes, meatballs, turmeric, salt and pepper. Half-cover the pan and cook over a gentle heat for 30 minutes, adding a little more water if necessary.

At the end of the cooking you should have a reasonable amount of sauce, which makes pasta an idea accompaniment for these meatballs.

Loubia

WHITE KIDNEY BEANS WITH BEEF AND CUMIN

Preparation ✦ 15 minutes
Cooking ✦ 2 hours

500 g/1 lb white kidney beans, soaked overnight
500 g/1 lb diced shin of beef
1 bulb of garlic
1 tbsp vegetable oil
1 tbsp mild paprika

1 tbsp cumin
Salt
Pepper

Put the beef and kidney beans into a large saucepan together with the garlic, oil and paprika. Add enough water to cover the ingredients and simmer for an hour and a half, adding a little more water if necessary. Five minutes before the end of the cooking, season with salt and pepper and, just before serving, stir in the cumin.

This is a very simple dish and, at the same time, a meal in itself. To vary it, my mother would sometimes use 3 or 4 *merguez* – spicy beef sausages – cut in half, instead of the beef. The *merguez* give the dish a slightly hotter but equally delicious flavour.

Ragoût de Foie

LIVER STEW WITH CUMIN

Preparation ✦ 15 minutes
Cooking ✦ 30 minutes

500 g / 1 lb calf's or lamb's liver
5 cloves of garlic, crushed
500 g / 1 lb small potatoes
1 tsp cumin
1 tsp mild paprika
2 tbsp wine vinegar
A small bunch of coriander
3 tbsp vegetable oil
Salt
Pepper

Brown the liver quickly for 2 minutes each side under a hot grill, then allow it to cool just enough so that you can cut it into thick slices. Now lightly crush the garlic with a pestle and mortar – this releases more flavour than chopping the garlic – and fry it with the oil in a saucepan until golden. Add the paprika, cumin, salt, pepper and the potatoes. Pour in 2 glasses of water, cook for 20 minutes and then add the liver and the vinegar. Add the chopped coriander and simmer, covered, and after 10 minutes it's ready.

Cervelle à la Sauce au Piment Rouge

BRAIN IN A PAPRIKA SAUCE

Preparation ✦ 10 minutes
Cooking ✦ 30 minutes

1 calf's brain
4 tsp wine vinegar
5 cloves of garlic
2 tbsp vegetable oil
1 tbsp mild paprika
A bunch of coriander
3 eggs
Salt
Pepper

Wash the brain in cold running water, pull off the membrane and boil it for 10 minutes in water to which you have added the wine vinegar.

Then, handling the brain very carefully, cut it into 1 inch cubes and put them in a saucepan with the oil. Add half the coriander, the garlic, paprika, salt and pepper, pour in a glass of water and cook slowly, covered, for 25 minutes.

Five minutes before the end of the cooking break the eggs, one by one, into the sauce and let them poach. Add the rest of the chopped coriander just before serving.

Brain may no longer be bought in Britain, but it is still sold throughout the rest of Europe and in North America and it's well worth making this typically *pied noir* dish anywhere that the principal ingredient is safe to eat and is to be found in butchers' shops.

Schkemba

TRIPE WITH PAPRIKA, CUMIN AND POTATOES

Preparation ✦ 30 minutes
Cooking ✦ 3 hours

1 kg / 2 lb tripe
6-8 cloves of garlic
1 tsp paprika, hot or mild
3 tbsp vegetable oil
1 tsp cumin
500 g / 1 lb potatoes, cut into quarters
3 tbsp red wine vinegar
A bunch of fresh coriander
Salt
Pepper

Buy the tripe already cleaned and boiled – this is much easier than doing these two jobs yourself.

Cut the cleaned and boiled tripe into 1 inch cubes and mix it in a saucepan with the crushed garlic, paprika, salt and pepper. Then add enough water to cover the tripe and cook over a medium heat for 2 hours, adding a little more water if necessary.

After 2 hours add the oil, cumin, vinegar and the potatoes. Reduce the heat and cook for another hour, after which you should have a thick, rich sauce. Add the chopped coriander just before serving.

Côtelettes d'Agneau aux Fèves et Coeurs d'Artichauts

LAMB CHOPS WITH BROAD BEANS AND ARTICHOKE HEARTS

Preparation ✦ 20 minutes
Cooking ✦ 1 hour 45 minutes

1 ½ kg / 3 lb lamb chops
750 g / 1 ½ lb fresh broad beans
3 cloves of garlic, crushed
1 tsp ginger
A pinch of saffron
3 tbsp vegetable oil
1 tin artichoke hearts or 4 fresh artichoke hearts,
cut into quarters
1 tbsp lemon juice
Salt
Pepper

Begin by washing and shelling the broad beans, and remember to put a dozen empty pods to one side – adding these at a later stage to the sauce is a trick of my mother's which makes for a heartier dish.

Next, heat the oil in a large pan and fry the garlic until golden. Add the lamb chops, stir them in with the garlic and then add the ginger, saffron, salt and pepper. Put just enough water into the pan to cover the chops and simmer them, covered, for about 1 hour, after which the meat should be very tender.

If you are using fresh artichokes, separate the hearts following the instructions on p.30 and blanch them. Then add the quartered artichoke hearts, the empty pods, the beans themselves, the lemon juice and, if necessary, a little more water.

Cook on a gentle heat for another 30 minutes, still covered, after which you should have a rich sauce.

Chicken

MY MOTHER HAD a little trick when it came to buying chicken, which are still sold live in the *souks* and killed to order. Before choosing a bird, she would bend down close enough to blow on the feathers and look at the skin to make certain that it was pink. Then she would inspect the bird's feet – she wanted to check the length of its claws, knowing that the older birds, which had tougher meat, had longer claws. Finally, she would inspect the gullet, looking to find whole corn kernels there, a sure sign that the bird had been corn-fed.

Once that was done and a price agreed upon, there came the part that I never grew to like – the seller would cut the bird's throat, bleeding it according to Islamic law. The chicken was then wrapped in paper and we would carry it home.

The maid would spend half an hour plucking the feathers, after which my mother would cut off the head and feet, clean the insides and light the stove. She would then take the bird in both hands and hold it a foot or so above the flame – this was the easiest and most efficient way of burning off whatever small feathers were left unplucked.

The liver, kidneys and heart were fried with onions for eating later that day. If we were really lucky, the rest of the bird was turned into the dish I loved best, *poulet aux olives*.

Poulet aux Olives

CHICKEN WITH OLIVES

Preparation ✦ 30 minutes
Cooking ✦ 1 hour 30 minutes

A chicken weighing 1½ kg / 3 lb
1 large onion, chopped
2 tomatoes, skinned and chopped
4 small potatoes, halved
3 cloves of garlic, chopped
3 tbsp olive oil
5 mushrooms, sliced
250 g / 8 oz green olives, pitted
1 tsp mild paprika
1 tbsp thyme
1 bay leaf
Salt
Pepper

Wash the chicken thoroughly, cut it into pieces and fry them in olive oil in a large pan. After 10 minutes add the onion, potatoes, tomatoes, garlic, bay leaf, thyme, paprika, salt, pepper and enough water to cover all the ingredients.

Now cover the pot and cook on a medium heat for 1 hour,

after which the chicken should be very tender. While the chicken is cooking, blanche the olives in boiling water for 5 minutes so that there's no risk of them making the sauce too salty. Reduce the heat, add the olives and the mushrooms and cook for a further 20 minutes, by which time the sauce will begin to thicken.

In Casablanca, where fresh mushrooms weren't readily available, my mother used *champignons de Paris* which came in a little tin. When we got to France, she of course used fresh mushrooms, which were easy to find.

Poulet au Citron et aux Olives

CHICKEN WITH LEMON AND OLIVES

Preparation ✦ 20 minutes
Cooking ✦ 1 hour

A chicken weighing 1½ kg / 3 lb
3 preserved lemons, cut into thin slices (see p. 139)
3 tbsp vegetable oil
1 onion, finely chopped
3 cloves of garlic
200 g / 7 oz purple olives, pitted
½ tsp saffron
A bunch of coriander
Salt
Pepper

Cut the chicken into pieces, brown them in oil in a large pan and put to one side.

Add the onion, garlic, saffron, salt and pepper to the same pan, stirring over a medium heat for 5 minutes before returning the chicken pieces to the pan together with enough water to cover all the ingredients.

Continue cooking, covered, until the chicken is tender, which should take about 45 minutes. While the chicken is cooking, blanche the olives in boiling water for 5 minutes and, when the chicken has cooked for about 30 minutes, add them and the slices of preserved lemon to the sauce. Scatter over the chopped coriander just before serving.

If you haven't made the preserved lemons yourself – and remember, you need to make them a couple of weeks in advance – they can be bought in North African shops.

Poulet aux Coings

CHICKEN WITH QUINCES

Preparation ◆ 30 minutes
Cooking ◆ 1 hour 30 minutes

A chicken weighing 1 1/2 kg / 3 lb
500 g / 1 lb quinces
2 onions, thinly sliced
3 tbsp vegetable oil
1 tsp ginger
1 tsp mild paprika
1 tbsp cinnamon
1 tsp honey
A small bunch of coriander
Juice of half a lemon
Salt
Pepper

Cut the chicken into pieces. Heat the oil in a large pan and fry them, adding the onion, paprika, ginger, salt, pepper and finally just enough water to cover everything. Cook, covered, over a medium heat for 20 minutes, turning the pieces of chicken after 10 minutes.

Meanwhile, wash, quarter and core the quinces, but do not peel them. Then put the quinces into the pan with the chicken, adding a glass of water, the honey, cinnamon and lemon juice. Cook, covered, over a low heat for another 20 minutes, by when you should have a rich sauce.

Continue to cook, still covered, on a low heat for another 20 minutes, then add the chopped coriander and transfer to a serving dish.

Poulet aux Pois-Chiches, Oeufs et Paprika

CHICKEN WITH CHICK-PEAS, EGGS AND PAPRIKA

Preparation ✦ 30 minutes
Cooking ✦ 2 hours

A chicken weighing 1 1/2 kg / 3 lb
250 g / 8 oz dried chick-peas, soaked overnight
5 cloves of garlic, unchopped
1 tsp mild paprika
3 tbsp vegetable oil
4 eggs
1 tsp cumin
Salt
Pepper

This Sephardi recipe, with its typically Spanish combination of chick-peas and paprika, is traditionally made by Algerian Jews on the night of Yom Kippur.

Drain the chick-peas, which must be soaked overnight. Then cover them with fresh water, add the paprika and garlic, which should be peeled but not chopped, bring to the boil and cook, covered, on a low heat for an hour and a half. You will have to add a little more water every now then.

While the chick-peas are cooking, cut the chicken into pieces and brown them in oil. When the chick-peas are almost tender, lay the pieces of chicken on top of them. Continue to cook for 10 minutes before breaking the eggs over the chicken and chick-peas. Mix well, cook for one more minute, add the cumin, salt and pepper and serve.

La Pastilla d'Henriette

PASTILLA

Preparation ✦ 1 hour
Cooking ✦ 1 hour 30 minutes

A chicken weighing 2 kg / 4 lb
4 large onions, finely chopped
2 tbsp vegetable oil
250 g / 8 oz almonds
5 eggs
1 tsp cinnamon
5 tsp castor sugar
200 g / 7 oz raisins
24 sheets of filo pastry
Vegetable oil for deep-frying
Salt

Most people who know the cuisine of North Africa think of *pastilla* or *bistilla* as a pigeon pie covered with very thin sheets of home-made puff pastry. Glazed with egg, it is cooked on charcoal and half-way through transferred to a large pan so that it can be cooked on the other side. It is still made this way in expensive restaurants, where the owner impresses tourists by bringing it out, with all the appropriate pomp and circumstance, two feet in diameter and with the pastry stacked forty sheets high.

But *pastilla* is just as often made at home with chicken, seafood or vegetable fillings. This is a modern recipe, named for my sister's mother-in-law, who first learned how to make it when growing up in Fez. She has since adapted it, simplifying the process and bringing it more in line with today's style of cooking.

Boil the chicken in a large saucepan over a medium heat until it is very tender. This should take around 45 minutes. When it's done, remove the bird from the water and allow it to cool – and make sure that you save the stock for use later.

Once the chicken has cooled, take the meat off the bones, cut it into small pieces and put them into a mixing bowl. Lightly brown the onions in a frying pan and add them to the chicken.

Blanch the almonds following the instructions on p.100 and, when they're dry, grill them until they're golden brown. Then put them in a food-processor and cut them into tiny pieces, but take care to stop short of reducing them to a powder. Add them to the chicken and onion mixture.

Beat the eggs and mix them into 1 pint of the stock that you have kept from cooking the chicken. Heat this in a saucepan over a medium heat, taking care not to let it boil, add salt and mix well with a wooden spoon for 3 minutes. Then pour this into the mixing bowl, adding the sugar, cinnamon and raisins.

Normally this dish is served as one large pie – Henriette's variation is to form it into small, individual portions, exactly like the *beztels* (p.20). Heat the oil for deep-frying and cook the *pastillas* until they are a light gold colour, turning them once. Drain on a paper towel and serve either hot or cold.

La Paella

PAELLA

Preparation ✦ 30 minutes
Cooking ✦ 45 minutes

8 chicken legs
2 chorizo sausages, sliced
4 tbsp olive oil
1 onion, chopped
3 cloves of garlic, chopped
200 g / 7 oz long-grain rice
½ tsp saffron
1 tomato, skinned and sliced
1 bay leaf
1 red pepper, grilled and cut into small slices
150 g / 5 oz peas
2 artichoke hearts, cut into quarters
500 g / 1 lb peeled prawns
A bunch of parsley
Salt
Pepper

The Iberian roots of many *pieds noirs* are obvious in our version of Spain's national dish. The Spanish, however, always serve paella from the pan in which it has cooked, and which gives the dish its name, while we transfer ours to a serving dish.

Start by frying the chicken and the *chorizos* in a large saucepan with 3 tablespoons of the olive oil. When they're brown, take them out and put them to one side.

Using the same pan over a medium heat, add another tablespoon of olive oil, the onion, garlic, tomato, bay leaf, peas, artichoke hearts, saffron, the rice, salt and pepper. Add enough water to cover the ingredients, cover, reduce the heat and cook for about 30 minutes. Every ten minutes or so you'll need to check the juice in which everything is cooking and, if it is evaporating too quickly, add a little more. Whatever happens, you don't want the rice and vegetables to dry out and stick to the bottom of the pan.

While this is cooking, grill the prawns for 5 minutes and also grill, skin, seed and stem the red pepper as in the recipe for *frita* (p.31) and cut it into small pieces.

When the rice is ready – again, the whole process should take 30 minutes – add the prawns and pepper to taste, allowing the dish to continue cooking until the juice is almost all absorbed. This usually takes just another few minutes. At this point, add the chicken, *chorizo* and grilled red pepper and allow to cook for 5 more minutes.

Transfer the paella to a big dish, using the prawns to decorate the rice, and sprinkle with the chopped parsley before serving.

Fish

THE IMPORTANCE OF FISH in our cuisine is easily understood, as Morocco has both Mediterranean and Atlantic coastlines. Casablanca is the country's most important fishing port and a huge variety of fish is landed there every day. This abundance is found at other ports, and especially at Tangiers, where, like Casablanca, the morning markets teem with sardines, pandora, whiting, bream, king prawn, shrimp, tuna, crayfish, sea bass, sole, grouper, red mullet, grey mullet and squid.

It's not surprising, then, that we were introduced to fish as a regular part of our diet at a very early age. One of the things which I still find difficult to understand in both Northern Europe and North America is that some people are hesitant about cooking fish, not because they dislike its flavour or texture, but because they don't understand the variety of ways it can be used or because they complain that it leaves a lingering smell in the house. But the many ways fish can be used, together with the health benefits from eating fish regularly, far outweigh the disadvantage of occasionally needing to open the kitchen window after cooking.

Because we lived on the coast, we very rarely ate any freshwater fish. Nor did we eat shellfish, catfish or any of the so-called scavengers, none of which is kosher, but with the abundance and diversity of fish available to us, we were hardly deprived. My mother's philosophy where fish were concerned was that of experienced cooks everywhere. She never thought about which fish to cook until she'd been to the market to see what was available. Then, of course, she determined the freshness for herself, using all the usual tricks and looking out for the fish with the clearest eyes and the reddest gills.

Boulettes de Poisson

FISHBALLS IN TOMATO AND CORIANDER SAUCE

Preparation ✦ 20 minutes
Cooking ✦ 45 minutes

500 g / 1 lb whiting or sea bream, filleted
2 small onions
1 small tomato
1 potato, cut into quarters
125 g / 4 oz breadcrumbs
1 egg
2 tbsp tomato purée
2 tbsp olive oil
A pinch of nutmeg
1 bay leaf

A pinch of saffron
A bunch of coriander
Salt
Pepper

Rinse the fish well, put it into a food-processor with one of the onions and blend to a paste. Pour the mixture into a bowl and add half the chopped coriander, all the nutmeg, the breadcrumbs, the beaten egg, salt and pepper. Mix these ingredients together well with a wooden spoon and then, with wet hands, form fishballs the size of golfballs.

Meanwhile, heat the oil in a casserole and fry the second onion. When the onion is half-done, add the tomato, bay leaf, saffron, a pinch of salt and the pieces of potato. Cook them together over a medium heat, covered, for 15 minutes.

Now drop the fishballs into the sauce. Mix the tomato purée with 4 tablespoons of water and add it to the sauce, then simmer for 15 minutes, stirring occasionally. Add the rest of the finely chopped coriander and serve on a bed of rice or tiny star-shaped pasta.

Thon à la Catalane

TUNA WITH GHERKINS AND CAPERS IN TOMATO SAUCE

Preparation ✦ 15 minutes
Cooking ✦ 40 minutes

2 slices of fresh tuna weighing about 500 g / 1 lb each
500 g / 1 lb tomatoes, diced
1 onion, finely chopped
200 g / 7 oz small French-style gherkins ('cornichons'),
sliced in half lengthways

1 tbsp tomato purée, diluted in half a glass of water
2 tbsp capers
3 tbsp olive oil
1 tsp mild chilli powder
A small bunch of coriander
2 potatoes, cut into quarters
Salt
Pepper

We borrowed this one directly from our Spanish neighbours. They, however, had already added a North African touch to this classic recipe by using coriander in their version of this classic dish.

Fry the onion in a saucepan with olive oil until it is golden. Then add the diced tomatoes, tuna, tomato purée, potatoes, chilli powder, half the finely chopped coriander, capers, gherkins, salt and pepper. Pour in a little less than half a pint of water and cook over a gentle to medium heat, half-covered, for 30 minutes.

Five minutes before it's done, add the rest of the coriander.

Sardines à l'Escabèche

FRIED SARDINES WITH GARLIC AND VINEGAR

Preparation ✦ 15 minutes
Cooking ✦ 20 minutes

1 kg / 2 lb sardines
3 tbsp flour
6-8 tbsp olive oil
6-8 cloves of garlic

2 tbsp wine vinegar
2 tsp mild paprika
1 tsp mild chilli powder
1 tbsp cumin
A bunch of parsley
Salt
Pepper

Cut the heads off the sardines and clean them thoroughly. Then rinse them well, sprinkle with salt and pepper and roll them in the flour. Heat the oil in a pan and fry the sardines for a couple of minutes on each side, until done.

Put the fish to one side and, after allowing the pan to cool for 2-3 minutes, add a little more oil, together with the chopped garlic, paprika, cumin, chilli powder and a little more salt.

Cook the sauce for no more than 2 minutes, then add the vinegar and cook for another couple of minutes. Arrange the fish in a serving dish, pour over the sauce and sprinkle them with the chopped parsley.

One of the nice things about this dish is that it is equally tasty eaten hot or cold. In some parts of the world fresh sardines are only available during the summer months. If you can't find sardines, this recipe also works well with small mackerel.

Daurade aux Herbes

RED BREAM WITH HERBS

Preparation ✦ 30 minutes
Cooking ✦ 1 hour

A red bream, weighing about 2 kg / 5 lb

4 medium-sized potatoes, sliced
3 tomatoes, skinned and sliced
2 onions, sliced
5 carrots, sliced
2 lemons, peeled and sliced
A bunch of parsley
A bunch of coriander
1 small glass of white wine
3 tbsp olive oil
1 tsp mild paprika
1 tsp thyme
1 bay leaf
Salt
Pepper

First, the fish must be scaled and cleaned. Then pre-heat your oven to 200°C/400°F/gas mark 6 and place the fish in a large baking dish, sprinkle it with salt and pepper, prick the fish on both sides with a fork and arrange the onions, tomatoes, potatoes, carrots and lemon around it. Cover the fish with the chopped parsley and coriander and top it off with the bay leaf. Now dribble the oil and scatter the paprika, thyme, salt and pepper over the fish and pour the wine over it and the vegetables.

Cover with aluminium foil and bake for half an hour, basting from time to time.

Then remove the foil and cook for a further half-hour, still basting the fish occasionally.

The dish works perfectly well on its own, although some people enjoy it with a little *aïoli*. To make this rich garlicky sauce, simply mix 6 tablespoons of home-made mayonnaise (p.37) with a couple of cloves of finely chopped garlic.

Rougets Frits

FRIED RED MULLET

Preparation ✦ 10 minutes
Cooking ✦ 15 minutes

1 kg / 2 lb red mullet
6 tbsp olive oil
Juice of 2 lemons
3 tbsp flour
Salt
Pepper

This is one of those recipes that, while not being specifically *pied noir*, was popular because the principal ingredient, red mullet, was so plentiful in the markets. We adopted it as our own in North Africa and brought it back with us to France, where it remains a favourite with *pied noir* families.

Wash and clean the fish thoroughly, but do not cut off the heads. Dry them with kitchen paper, sprinkle with salt and pepper and roll them in the flour, shaking off any excess.

Heat the oil in a large frying pan and, only when it is very hot, add the fish. They will fry quickly. The moment they turn a light brown colour, remove them from the pan, place them in a serving dish and add the salt, pepper and lemon juice.

The simplest of dishes, it goes very well with boiled cauliflower, leeks, potatoes and carrots served in a vinaigrette.

Calmars Sauce Paprika

SQUID IN PAPRIKA SAUCE

Preparation + 20 minutes
Cooking + 45 minutes

1 1/2 kg / 3 lb squid
1 large onion, sliced
5 cloves of garlic, finely chopped
2 mild chillis
4 tbsp olive oil
2 tomatoes, diced
1 glass of white wine
1 tbsp tomato purée, diluted in a small amount of water
1 tsp mild paprika
1 tsp thyme
1 tsp rosemary
1 bay leaf
Salt
Pepper

The squid must be cleaned, with the contents of the sac removed, as well as the hard beak-like nose and the eyes. It's probably easiest to ask your fishmonger to do this and also to slice the body into rings and the tentacles into small lengths.

Heat the oil in a pan and fry the onion until it is translucent, then add the garlic, tomatoes, chillis, paprika, bay leaf, thyme and rosemary. Put the squid pieces in the sauce, add the tomato purée, the wine, salt, pepper and a glass of water.

Keep it half-covered, over a medium heat, for 45 minutes. Generally speaking, that should be enough, but squid must be tender and, if you need another few minutes, don't rush them. Serve with wild rice.

An interesting variation, a favourite of my sister in New York, is to substitute prawns for squid and then add parsley. She cooks them for only 15 minutes.

Mérou au Piment Rouge et Sauce Coriandre

GROUPER WITH PIMENTO IN CORIANDER SAUCE

Preparation ✦ 15 minutes
Cooking ✦ 45 minutes

1 kg/2 lb grouper, cut into slices
3-4 dried red peppers or ñoras
3 potatoes, sliced
2 tomatoes
5 cloves of garlic
A bunch of coriander
1 tsp mild paprika
4 tbsp olive oil
Salt
Pepper

Combine the oil, garlic, fish, finely chopped coriander, ñoras, potatoes and tomatoes in a large pan over a medium heat. Add salt and pepper, cover with water and then stir in the paprika. Half-cover the pan and cook for 45 minutes.

Ñoras are small, fat, red peppers that have been dried in sun – they can be found in most Spanish and Arab food shops and in some delicatessens. Ordinary dried red peppers will work for this recipe, but ñoras have a particular taste and we always use them to make *mérou au piment rouge*.

If grouper isn't available, monkfish or sea bream can be used to make this dish.

Poisson Sauce Chermoula

FISH IN CHERMOULA SAUCE

Preparation ✦ 1 hour 20 minutes
Cooking ✦ 1 hour

For the sauce
5 cloves of garlic, crushed with 2 tsp salt
A bunch of fresh coriander, finely chopped
A bunch of fresh parsley, finely chopped
5 tbsp olive oil
A small pinch of saffron
1 tsp mild chilli powder
1 tsp mild paprika
1/4 tsp hot chilli powder
2 tsp ground cumin seeds
3 tbsp lemon juice
3 tbsp water
Salt

For the fish
A whole sea bream weighing about 1 1/2 kg/3 lb
3 tomatoes, sliced
2 green peppers, seeded and sliced
1 preserved lemon, peeled and cut into strips
2 tbsp flour (optional, for frying)
4 tbsp olive oil (optional, for frying)

Slightly different versions of this delicious sauce are made in every village, almost even in every home in Morocco. This is one of those recipes that is passed from mother to daughter and adapted to the tastes of each family. A highly seasoned sauce, it combines parsley, garlic, coriander, cumin, saffron and olive oil, and by playing with the balance of the ingredients you'll undoubtedly find a variation to suit your own taste. This is the version I cook for my family and it goes particularly well with fried whiting fillets or red snapper or baked or poached halibut, sea bream or sea bass. The fish can be cooked whole or cut into fillets or steaks.

The one catch to this recipe is that you need to have made the preserved lemon in advance. Preserved lemons take only a quarter of an hour to prepare, but they need to have sat in a jar for three weeks – see p.139. If you don't have any preserved lemons to hand, they can be bought in Middle Eastern food shops.

By contrast, making the sauce is both simple and quick – you simply combine all the ingredients in a large bowl.

Place the fish in a baking dish; pour half the *chermoula* sauce over the fish and leave it to marinate for 1 hour, turning it from time to time.

Discard the pulp from the preserved lemon, cut its skin into strips and arrange these with the sliced tomatoes, green peppers and the fish. Now pour the rest of the *chermoula* sauce over the fish and cover the dish with foil to bake in an oven pre-heated to 190°C/375°F/gas mark 5 for 30 minutes.

Then reduce the oven temperature to 150°C/300°F/gas mark 2, remove the foil, baste the fish, adding a little water if necessary, and return it to the oven for another 30 minutes.

If you prefer to fry the fish, make the sauce in exactly the same way. Marinate the fish for 1 hour in the sauce, remove any excess with a paper towel, dip the fish in the flour and fry it in a large pan in very hot olive oil until it is golden brown.

Once you have removed any excess oil from the fish, put it on a serving plate and simply pour over the uncooked sauce.

Tagines

A *TAGINE* IS A STEW which takes its name from the earthenware pot with a conical lid in which it is cooked. Every *pied
noir* household in Morocco owned several of these ceramic
pots in a variety of sizes. At home we referred to our smallest
tagine – which wasn't particularly small – as *la famille*, in
which my mother could cook a stew for the eight of us who
made up our immediate family. The next size up we called
les tantes, brought out when our aunts, uncles and cousins
came to dinner. Then there was *le roi*, for our version of royal
banquets, when distant cousins joined closer relations,
neighbours and friends. Once the stew was cooked, it was
brought to the table in the pot with the conical lid still on
top – the *tagine* became the serving dish – and great ceremony was made of uncovering the dish.

   Under the lid would be a steaming stew. There might be
lamb, beef or chicken seasoned with coriander, saffron,

paprika, cumin and ginger and then simmered very slowly with preserved lemons, tomatoes, almonds, olives, chick-peas, onions and other vegetables. Wealthy families made pigeon *tagines*, while poorer families stuck to vegetable *tagines*. Nowadays, fish *tagines* are to be found on the menu in some Moroccan restaurants, but neither *pieds noirs* nor Moroccan Arabs are known for their fish *tagines* – for whatever reason, Tunisians are much keener on fish dishes than Moroccans.

Stalls in the *souks* are piled high with *tagines* and they are inexpensive. A new *tagine* needs to be prepared before cooking in it for the first time. My mother would combine the ingredients of what was, in effect, a vegetable stock. She filled the *tagine* with a couple of peeled onions, a few carrots, a couple of bay leaves, some thyme and rosemary, four or five cloves of garlic, some olive oil and water. The *tagine* would then be covered with its lid and placed in a pre-heated oven set on a low heat. She would leave it there for at least an hour, long enough for the flavours to spread throughout the inside of the *tagine*. Then she would take the *tagine* out of the oven and allow it to cool overnight before throwing away the stock. The next day she repeated the procedure, just to make certain that the *tagine* was ready. I was always upset that the stock went down the drain, because it smelled so good, but the idea was to remove any earthenware odours from the *tagine* and to impregnate it with a particular flavour.

Those who don't have a *tagine* can still make these stews in a large casserole dish. Any large earthenware pot will do, as long as you can use it over a low heat and inside the oven.

COOKING WITH ALMONDS

Moroccan cooking is famous for its use of almonds, which are skinned and blanched before being added to stews or pastries. Nowadays they are generally bought pre-blanched in Europe and North America, but they retain a much sweeter milkiness if bought unskinned and then blanched just before use. In the *souks* they were only to be found complete with their skins, and they can still be bought like this in supermarkets in the West.

Blanching almonds is both quick and easy. Bring a pan of water to a vigorous boil, remove it from the heat and immediately drop in the almonds. Stir, cover the pan and leave for 3-4 minutes. Test a nut to see that the skin is easily removed by squeezing it between your fingers and thumb. If the nuts are ready, drain off the hot water and cool them in cold running water. After squeezing off the skins, rinse them again in cold water and dry them thoroughly with a tea-towel.

Poulet aux Pruneaux et aux Amandes

CHICKEN WITH PRUNES AND ALMONDS

Preparation ✦ 20 minutes
Cooking ✦ 1 hour 30 minutes

A chicken weighing about 1½ kg / 3 lb
2 large onions
4 or 5 tbsp ground almonds
3 tbsp olive oil
20 prunes, pitted and soaked for 2 hours
1 tbsp mild paprika
Salt
Pepper

The French have absorbed a number of dishes from our cuisine into their repertoire, but *tagines* have not become a part of their cooking in the way that couscous has, probably because combining fruit with meat is something they do only rarely. However fruit can be an excellent complement to meat and I happily admit to having a soft spot for *tagines*, like this one, which bring the sweetness and soft texture of fruit together with meat.

First of all, soak the prunes in cold water for a couple of hours before you begin to prepare the rest of the dish.

Rinse the chicken, cut it into small pieces and set it aside. Now brown the onions, which should be very finely sliced, in a frying pan and, when they're ready, add the chicken pieces.

Once the chicken is tender, transfer it and the onions to a *tagine* or casserole, add the prunes, salt, pepper, paprika, the ground almonds and enough of the water in which you soaked the prunes to cover all the ingredients. Stir well, then cover the pot and allow the stew to simmer over a low heat for one hour.

Serve in the *tagine*.

Poulet aux Abricots

CHICKEN WITH APRICOTS

Preparation ◆ 30 minutes
Cooking ◆ 1 hour

1 chicken, cut into 6 pieces
2 sliced onions
500 g/1 lb apricots, soaked overnight
75 g/2 ½ oz butter
1 tbsp honey

½ tsp cinnamon
½ tsp ginger
A small pinch of saffron
Salt

This terrific variation on the previous recipe combines chicken with apricots, but this time the *tagine* is cooked in the oven rather than on the stove.

The secret of this dish lies in the apricots, and they must be soaked overnight so that they become very soft when cooked.

Brown the onion and the chicken with the butter in a frying pan over a medium heat. Line the *tagine* or casserole with the soaked apricots, pour in 1 pint of cold water and then add the chicken pieces and the onions. Season with the salt, ginger and saffron.

Now pour in the honey and add the cinnamon, stirring constantly to mix the honey around each piece of chicken, but always keeping the apricots on the bottom. Add just enough water at this point to immerse the chicken fully. Then cover the pot. Don't worry if you are using a casserole without a lid, as aluminum foil will do – just remember to poke a few holes in the foil to allow the steam to escape.

Put the *tagine* or casserole into an oven pre-heated to 150°C/300°F/gas mark 2 so that the stew can cook slowly for about 45-50 minutes – you'll know that the chicken is done by poking the meat with a fork and seeing that it's tender.

When it's ready, bring the *tagine* to the table. This dish goes well with plain white rice and a green salad.

Mouton aux Poires

LAMB WITH PEARS

Preparation ✦ 30 minutes
Cooking ✦ 2 hours

1 kg / 2 lb diced leg of lamb
2 large onions, chopped
150 g / 5 oz almonds
2 tbsp olive oil
1 tsp cinnamon
1 tsp ginger
½ tsp saffron
A bunch of coriander
4 pears, peeled, cored and cut into small pieces
Salt
Pepper

Pour the olive oil into the *tagine*, put it over a medium heat and, when the oil is hot, add the onion. As soon as the onion starts to turn translucent, reduce the heat and add the meat, the cinnamon, ginger, saffron, chopped coriander, salt and pepper and just enough water to cover the meat.

Cover and simmer gently until the meat is tender, for about an hour and a half. Meanwhile, blanch and skin the almonds following the instructions on p.100 and add them to the *tagine*, together with the pears.

Cook for a further 30 minutes, or long enough to soften the pears, and serve.

This dish works almost as well with apples and quinces and takes the same amount of time to cook.

Mouton aux Tomates et aux Amandes

LAMB WITH TOMATOES AND ALMONDS

Preparation ✦ 30 minutes
Cooking ✦ 2 hours

1½ kg/3 lb diced shoulder of lamb
5 tbsp olive oil
2 onions, finely chopped
2 cloves of garlic, finely chopped
1 tsp cinnamon
1 tsp ginger
½ tsp saffron
6 tomatoes, skinned, seeded and chopped
200 g/7 oz almonds
Salt
Pepper

Brown the onion in the *tagine* and then add the garlic. Put the meat on top of the onion and garlic and season with the cinnamon, ginger, saffron, salt and pepper. Now add the tomatoes and just enough water to cover the meat.

Bring to the boil and then simmer for about an hour and a half or until the meat is tender. While the lamb is cooking, blanch and skin the almonds following the instructions on p.100. Then brown them lightly under a hot grill and add them to the *tagine* just before serving.

Agneau aux Pruneaux avec Sésame et Amandes

LAMB WITH PRUNES, SESAME SEEDS AND ALMONDS

Preparation ✦ 30 minutes
Cooking ✦ 2 hours

1½ kg/3 lb diced shoulder of lamb
500 g/1 lb prunes, soaked overnight
2 onions, finely chopped
3 cloves of garlic, finely chopped
2 tsp cinnamon
1 tsp ginger
5 tbsp vegetable oil
150 g/5 oz almonds
4 tbsp sesame seeds, lightly toasted
5 tbsp sugar
Salt

Place the pieces of lamb in the *tagine* or a large casserole and add the oil, one of the onions, the garlic, one of the teaspoons of cinnamon, the ginger and salt. Cover with water, bring gently to the boil and then simmer over a medium heat for about 30 minutes. As soon as the juice comes to the boil, take off two ladles and put to one side.

Blanch and skin the almonds following the instructions on p.100. Dry and then fry them in a tablespoon of hot vegetable oil until golden.

Toasting the sesame seeds is very simple. You can either line a baking dish with a sheet of aluminium foil, spread out the seeds and place them under a grill until they toast, or sprinkle them into a hot frying pan, without oil, and gently shake the pan while they toast. Neither process will take longer than 2 or 3 minutes. You will, however, need to keep an eye on them so that they don't burn.

Now, when the meat is tender, add the second onion and, at the same time, 2 tablespoons of the sugar. Continue to cook for about another 15 minutes, stirring constantly.

Put the juice from cooking the lamb that you set to one side into a saucepan and cook the prunes in it for about 15 minutes, than add 3 tablespoons of sugar and the other teaspoon of cinnamon, simmering until the sugar is well absorbed by the prunes. Remove the saucepan from the heat and put to one side.

Place the meat in a large serving dish, add the prunes, pour over the sauce and garnish with the fried almonds and toasted sesame seeds.

Epaule d'Agneau aux Pruneaux

SHOULDER OF LAMB WITH PRUNES

Preparation ✦ 20 minutes
Cooking ✦ 2 hours

$1\frac{1}{2}$ kg / 3 lb diced shoulder of lamb
2 onions, finely chopped
250 g / 8 oz prunes, pitted and soaked for 2 hours
2 tbsp vegetable oil
$\frac{1}{4}$ tsp ginger
$\frac{1}{4}$ tsp nutmeg
125 g / 4 oz walnuts
1 tsp sugar
$\frac{1}{4}$ tsp cinnamon
Salt

Fry the onions in a large *tagine* until they're golden. Then add the meat and fry over a medium heat for another 5 minutes before adding the ginger, nutmeg, the prunes and salt. Cook for a further 10 minutes, then pour in enough water to cover the meat and prunes (or use the water in which the prunes have soaked), reduce the heat as low as you can and cook, covered, for an hour and half.

At this point, add the walnuts, sugar and cinnamon and simmer, still over a very low heat, for a final quarter of an hour.

Epaule d'Agneau à la Menthe

SHOULDER OF LAMB WITH MINT

Preparation ✦ 30 minutes
Cooking ✦ 1 hour 15 minutes

1 kg/2 lb diced shoulder of lamb
10 small onions
3 tomatoes, diced
1 lemon
A bunch of fresh mint
1 tsp thyme
6 tbsp vegetable oil
Salt
Pepper

First peel the onions and, leaving them whole, blanche them in boiling water for 3 minutes. Then, using half the oil, brown the onions in a frying pan. Now put the rest of the oil in a *tagine* and brown the diced lamb. Then add the tomatoes, onions, thyme, salt and pepper and a glass of water. Reducing the heat, cover the *tagine* and cook for an hour. If the sauce evaporates too quickly, add a little more water to keep the meat from burning.

While the lamb is cooking, juice half the lemon and peel and dice the other half. Five minutes before serving, add the diced lemon, lemon juice and the finely chopped mint.

Tagine de Légumes

VEGETABLE TAGINE

Preparation ✦ 20 minutes
Cooking ✦ 40 minutes

3 large potatoes, diced
3 carrots, diced
3 sticks of celery, diced
4-6 cloves of garlic
3 courgettes, peeled and diced
2 onions, chopped
1 mild chilli, finely chopped
3 tbsp olive oil
1 tsp cumin
A small bunch of parsley, finely chopped
Salt
Pepper

Start by bringing 2 pints of salted water to the boil, add the potatoes, carrots, celery, garlic and one of the onions and cook, uncovered, over a medium heat for 15 to 20 minutes, by when the vegetables should be tender. Five minutes before the other vegetables are done, add the courgettes.

While the other vegetables are cooking, gently fry the second onion and the chilli in an uncovered *tagine* and, when the onion is translucent, after 5 or 6 minutes, add the cumin, parsley, salt and pepper.

When the boiled vegetables are tender, transfer them to the *tagine* and mix them in with the onion and chilli. Cover the *tagine* and cook the combined vegetables for 10 minutes on a moderate heat so that the sauce thickens, adding a little more salt and pepper if necessary.

Couscous

COUSCOUS IS THE MOST TRADITIONAL of all *pied noir* dishes. Borrowed from the Arabs, it has become so much a part of our heritage that you might say that couscous is to the *pieds noirs* what pasta is to the Italians or rice to the Chinese.

The word couscous is derived from the Arabic '*kaskasa*', which means to pulverise, as the basis of the dish is small grains of semolina made from finely crushed wheat. This is steamed, usually over a meat and vegetable stew, and can be served with mutton, chicken, beef, fish or butter.

Typically, couscous was a Friday night meal, although it was also the special dish for family gatherings and celebration suppers. The ritual would begin the day before with the soaking of the chick-peas in water. Early the next morning we'd go off to the *souk* where my mother would choose tomatoes at one stall, onions at another and turnips at a third. Once my mother had bought all the meat and vegetables needed for the couscous, my maternal grand-mother would take over, spending the rest of the day preparing the grains, cooking everything slowly and with great care.

Perhaps the most difficult part of her preparation was the grain itself, because my grandmother would crush it and roll it by hand. In those days it was heresy even to consider using anything other than home-made couscous, but today, thank goodness, couscous grains are commercially prepared and available in supermarkets. They are as good as home-made grains and even a purist like my mother now admits that it is almost impossible to tell the difference.

Only one special cooking utensil is necessary in order to make couscous. In French this is known as a *couscoussier* and in English it would be called a very large steamer. The stew goes in the bottom half and the grain sits in the top half where it cooks in the steam rising from the stew below. *Couscoussiers* can be bought from good kitchenware shops in Britain and North America.

Many people think of couscous as a very difficult and complex dish and I have lost count of the number of friends who, sitting down at our table for a couscous, express amazement when presented with a meal that they believe to be both time-consuming and complicated. In fact, making a couscous is no more difficult than making a soup, yet home-made couscous is always a memorable treat.

Traditionally, the Arabs make their couscous with *smen*, a type of preserved butter. I have not included *smen* in any of these recipes as it has never been used by *pied noir* cooks and, moreover, gives the couscous a slightly rancid taste which takes a lot of getting used to.

PREPARING COUSCOUS GRAINS

Preparation ✦ 15 minutes

1 kg/2 lb couscous grains
3 tbsp vegetable oil
1 tsp salt
½ tsp pepper

Put the couscous grains into a very large bowl and sprinkle them with 2 pints of warm water and a teaspoon of salt. At the same time work the grains between your fingers until each is separated, moistened and beginning to swell.

Leave them to stand for 2 to 3 minutes, until all the water is absorbed, and then add the oil and the pepper and work the grains again until the oil too is well absorbed.

Couscous à la Viande et aux Légumes

COUSCOUS WITH MEAT AND VEGETABLES

Preparation ✦ 1 hour 30 minutes
Cooking ✦ 3 hours

1 kg/2 lb couscous
3 tbsp vegetable oil
✦
200 g/7 oz chick-peas, soaked overnight
750 g/1½ lb shin of beef
500 g/1 lb shoulder of lamb
2 marrow bones
3 onions
4 tomatoes

4 turnips
1 kg/2 lb courgettes
500 g/1 lb pumpkin, skinned and cubed
A stick of celery
A white cabbage, cored and cut into quarters
3 tbsp of vegetable oil
A small bunch of coriander
1 tsp mild paprika
A couple of pinches of saffron
Salt
Pepper

When making couscous you must always use dried chick-peas which have to be soaked overnight – they're to be cooked for such a long time that tinned chick-peas, which are pre-cooked, would simply disintegrate.

Peel the onions, tomatoes and turnips and cut them into small pieces. Now cut the courgettes in half lengthways, then in half again, this time widthways.

Pour the oil into the bottom half of the *couscoussier* and brown the meat, which should be left on the bone, for 10 minutes on a high heat. Then add the onions, tomatoes, salt and pepper, stirring frequently so that the vegetables don't stick and burn. After 10 minutes reduce the heat, add 4 pints of cold water, the chick-peas and the marrow bones and leave to cook on a medium heat.

After 1 hour add the turnips, celery, cabbage, pumpkin cubes and paprika to the broth, together with another pint of water. Reduce to a low heat and allow to simmer.

While the meat and vegetables are cooking, prepare the couscous grains as in the instructions preceding this recipe. When the stew has cooked for a further 1 hour and 10 minutes, put the couscous grains in the top half of the steamer and place them, covered, over the broth. They will stay there for the final 30 minutes of cooking. Stir the grains every 10 minutes or so to spread the moisture evenly. This is the single most important point to remember about making couscous, as the grains must never be allowed to stick together.

After the grains have been cooking for a quarter of an hour, add the courgettes, a couple of pinches of saffron and the chopped coriander. You may, depending on your taste, want to add a little more salt and pepper to the broth. Simmer for another 15 minutes before serving.

VARIATIONS

Couscous is one of those dishes, like risotto, that offers a great many variations on a theme and there are innumerable combinations of meat, fish, fowl and vegetables that you can try once you have mastered the basic method. These are a few of the more common variations.

Couscous aux Boulettes uses the meatballs prepared for the *chou farci* (p.44) and substitutes them for the shin of beef.

Couscous au Poulet uses pieces of chicken – which must be fried first – instead of the shoulder of lamb.

Additional vegetables can be added, depending on the season and personal taste. There are already seven vegetables in my mother's basic couscous, but that doesn't mean there isn't room for more. I usually add half a dozen carrots and I know people who also put in a couple of aubergines. The carrots are peeled and cut into quarters, while aubergines should be trimmed and halved lengthways. Both go into the broth at the same time as the turnips, celery, cabbage and pumpkin.

SERVING THE COUSCOUS

There are two distinct philosophies when it comes to bringing couscous to the table. The first holds that the different elements of the meal should be presented separately. There is one serving dish for the grain, another for the meat and vegetables and a third for the broth.

The other is to use one really big plate which you cover with the couscous, dousing it with just enough broth to moisten the grains and then build a small mound on top with the vegetables and chick-peas. Whichever way you serve the couscous, the meat is presented separately, always in the broth in which it has cooked.

In either case, you begin by spooning a good helping of couscous grain onto everyone's plate, then adding *harissa*, a hot chilli sauce, to the grain. It is particularly important that the *harissa* be added at this point rather than passed round later, because you need the broth to dilute the *harissa* so that it doesn't overpower the dish.

Now serve the meat and the vegetables and, finally, pour over sufficient broth almost to cover everything.

You'll probably find that couscous is best eaten with a large spoon, accompanied by water. The French drink wine with couscous because they drink wine with everything, but we find that combining couscous with wine makes you much too thirsty.

Harissa

CHILLI SAUCE

Preparation ✦ 35 minutes

250 g/8 oz dried chillis
4 cloves of garlic
Salt

Couscous is always served with *harissa*, a hot sauce which can be bought in tins. Preparing it yourself, however, involves nothing more than soaking the dried chillis in water for half an hour, removing their stalks and seeds, adding the garlic, 3 tablespoons of water and a tablespoon of salt and blending everything to a fine paste.

Couscous Rouge aux Aubergines et Graines de Carvi

RED COUSCOUS WITH AUBERGINES AND CARAWAY SEEDS

Preparation ✦ 1 hour
Cooking ✦ 1 hour 15 minutes

1 kg/2 lb couscous
3 tbsp vegetable oil
✦
750 g/1½ lb diced shin of beef
3 large aubergines, peeled and cut into thirds
5 potatoes, cut into quarters
1 bulb of garlic, crushed

2 tbsp caraway seeds
6 tbsp vegetable oil
4 eggs
3 tomatoes, finely chopped
1 tbsp mild paprika
Salt
Pepper

Start by taking the garlic and crushing it in a mortar with the caraway seeds. Then heat the oil in the lower part of the *couscoussier* and add the meat together with the crushed garlic and caraway, stirring constantly. After 5 minutes add the tomatoes, paprika and the aubergines. Season with salt and pepper, pour in a pint and a half of water and cook over a medium heat for 30 minutes.

While the meat and vegetables are cooking, prepare the couscous following the instructions on p.112.

When the meat and vegetables have cooked for half an hour, add the potatoes and carefully lower the eggs, still in their shells, into the stew and put the couscous grains into the top part of the *couscoussier*. Cook on a medium heat for another 30 minutes. You'll have to check once or twice to make certain that there is enough water in the *couscoussier* to cover all the ingredients; if it begins to dry out, add a little more water.

A few minutes before the couscous is ready, remove the eggs and, after allowing them to cool, shell and slice them.

To serve, transfer the grains to a large serving dish, wet them with the broth, add the meat and vegetables and decorate with sliced hard-boiled eggs.

Couscous au Poisson

FISH COUSCOUS

Preparation ✦ 1 hour
Cooking ✦ 1 hour 30 minutes

1 kg / 2 lb couscous
3 tbsp vegetable oil
✦
1½ kg / 3 lb hake, cut into medium slices
125 g / 4 oz chick-peas, soaked overnight
3 tbsp vegetable oil
1 onion, chopped
2 small tomatoes, finely chopped
3 small turnips, cut into quarters
4 carrots, peeled and cut lengthways
5 small potatoes, cut into quarters
A stick of celery
A pinch of saffron
3 courgettes, cut into quarters
Salt
Pepper

I must confess that this is not a dish my mother ever made, although I've never been sure why, as Casablanca is a major port and we ate fish regularly. Oddly enough, it was my sister's mother-in-law, who was born and raised in the inland city of Fez, who taught me how to make this dish.

Heat the oil in the lower part of the *couscoussier*, then add the onion, tomatoes, chick-peas and 2 pints of water. Cook on a medium heat for 30 minutes before adding the carrots, turnips, celery, potatoes, saffron and 2 more pints of water.

While the chick-peas and vegetables are cooking, prepare the couscous following the instructions on p.112 and put them in the top half of the *couscoussier* after the vegetables have cooked for a further 30 minutes. At the same time add the fish to the chick-peas and vegetables, season with salt and pepper and cook for a further half-hour. Ten minutes before the end of the cooking you need to add the courgettes.

The fish will soften in the broth, so take care that when you take the slices out of the *couscoussier* they don't break up. Serve the fish on the same platter as the vegetables and the couscous. The broth is served separately.

Couscous au Beurre

BUTTERED COUSCOUS WITH SUGAR AND RAISINS

Preparation ✦ 30 minutes
Cooking ✦ 30 minutes

1 kg/2 lb couscous
3 tbsp vegetable oil
✦
250 g/8 oz unsalted butter
150 g/5 oz dried raisins, washed and drained
250 g/8 oz castor sugar
1 large pot of natural yoghurt
Salt
4 courgettes (optional)

This sweet dish is traditionally served by Algerian Jews on the last night of Passover in celebration of a festival called Mimouna.

A huge mound of buttered couscous was the centrepiece of a table laid out with sweets and cakes. Once the table was prepared, families would leave and make the rounds of neighbouring households, stopping by to taste the couscous and other delicacies they had on offer. On a good night you might visit a dozen other families, while those families also stopped by at your home. This was, of course, a way of reaffirming the bonds between families and friends and celebrating with a table laden with culinary treats.

Algerian Jews brought this dish with them to Casablanca, where we served it as a light meal – more often than not on a Sunday night after a weekend of heavy eating. *Couscous au beurre* is easy to make and, not surprisingly, a great favourite with children.

First of all, prepare the couscous following the instructions on p.112, but omitting the salt and pepper.

Steam the couscous over water for 10 minutes, then mix in the raisins and leave it to steam for another 10 minutes. Now toss the couscous the same way you would a salad to make sure the grains aren't sticking together and to ensure that the raisins are well mixed in with the couscous. Allow to steam for a final 10 minutes.

Pour the grains onto a large round plate – called a *k'sra* in Morocco, although a wok will do just as well – cut the butter into small pieces and add it to the couscous, tossing it to prevent lumps from forming. Finally, add a pinch of salt.

To serve, put the couscous onto a large plate and sprinkle it with sugar. Each guest gets a plateful of the sugared grains to which he or she adds yoghurt.

Some families, including mine, also add courgettes to this dish. We put them in the water in the bottom of the *couscoussier* for the last 10 minutes of the cooking and then eat them boiled, with a little salt, as a side dish. I have no idea where or why this practice originated, but it's something you often see in *pied noir* homes where a branch of the family has Algerian origins.

Traditionally, we drink a curdled buttermilk called *l'ben*, which is now available in most Middle Eastern food shops, with *couscous au beurre*.

Pastries and Breads

PASTRIES

In Morocco pastries are made to celebrate every possible special occasion – weddings, birthdays, anniversaries, family feasts and religious holidays – and also to eat with afternoon tea. Unlike the French, however, we rarely ate pastry as a dessert, as we normally finished a meal with fresh fruit. One reason for this might be that our pastries and cakes are slightly heavy, at least when compared to those found in most European cake shops. We don't use cream and hardly ever use butter in our pastries, a habit which possibly goes back to the Jewish prohibition on putting meat and dairy products together on the same table, and instead rely on walnuts, almonds, marzipan, honey, coconut, dried fruits, dates and figs.

Cigares aux Amandes

MARZIPAN CIGARS

Preparation ✦ 1 hour
Cooking ✦ 10 minutes for every 4 cigars
Makes 25-30

For the marzipan
250g/8oz almonds
200g/7oz sugar
1 egg
1 tsp orange flower water

For the cigars
250g/8oz flour
100ml/4floz white wine
100ml/4floz vegetable oil
1 tsp salt
1 egg-white
Vegetable oil for frying
250g/8oz clear honey

Start by making the marzipan. First of all, blanch and skin the almonds following the instructions on p.100. Then combine the blanched almonds with the sugar and the egg in a food-processor, pour in the orange flower water and mix until you have a stiff paste. This will give you a pound of marzipan.

To make the cigars, start by mixing the oil and the wine together – you'll have to stir them very briskly as they don't combine particularly easily. Then, a little at a time, pour the oil and wine mixture into the flour, to which you have already added the salt, kneading constantly so that you obtain a supple dough.

Place the dough on a floured surface, roll it out until it becomes very thin, sprinkle lightly with oil and then with a little flour.

Fold it in four, the way you would a piece of paper, roll it a second time, sprinkle with oil and flour once again and then roll it by hand into a long tube about 2 inches thick. Slice this into 1 inch lengths.

Now you must re-roll each of these slices to form the dough into narrow rectangles. Roll and cut the marzipan into short lengths and put one in the middle of each rectangle and then roll the dough around the marzipan to form it into a cigar shape. Use the egg-white like a glue to seal the edges on the inside flap.

Then heat the oil in a small saucepan, drop in the cigars, two by two, and fry them until they're a rich golden colour.

Heat the honey in another saucepan until it bubbles and, as soon as the cigars are cooked, drop them directly into the honey and leave them there for 2 minutes. Remove, transfer them to a plate, allow to cool and serve.

Gâteaux à la Noix de Coco

COCONUT CAKES

Preparation ✦ 20 minutes
Cooking ✦ 10 minutes
Makes about 25

2 egg-whites
250 g / 8 oz powdered coconut
125 g / 4 oz castor sugar

Beat the egg-whites in a bowl until they are stiff. Then gradually add the sugar and the coconut powder and form the mixture into small pyramids.

To bake, place a buttered pastry sheet on a tray and put the pyramids into an oven pre-heated to 180°C/350°F/gas mark 4 for 10 minutes, by when they should have turned a light brown.

Montecaos

CINNAMON CAKES

Preparation ✦ 15 minutes
Cooking ✦ 15 minutes
Makes 20-25

500 g / 1 lb flour
250 g / 8 oz castor sugar
200 ml / 7 fl oz vegetable oil
3 drops orange flower water
1 tbsp cinnamon

Place the flour in a mixing bowl and gradually add the sugar and then the oil and the orange flower water. Knead the dough with the palms of your hands until it softens and is no longer sticky.

On a floured surface, form the dough into cakes shaped like large prunes. Then flatten the centre of the top with your thumb and sprinkle a little cinnamon into this depression.

Arrange the cakes on a tray and bake them in an oven pre-heated to 180°C/350°F/gas mark 4 for 10-15 minutes, by when the *montecaos* should be a light gold colour.

Beztels aux Amandes

MARZIPAN BEZTELS

Preparation ✦ 30 minutes
Cooking ✦ 45 minutes
Makes about 30

For the marzipan
125 g / 4 oz almonds
100 g / 3 ½ oz sugar
Half an egg
½ tsp orange flower water

For the beztels
30 sheets of filo pastry
250 g / 8 oz clear honey
Vegetable oil for frying

First of all, make half a pound of marzipan following the instructions in the recipe for *cigares aux amandes* on p.122.

Then take the filo pastry, fold each sheet in half and then in half again. Put a scoop of marzipan on the edge of each sheet and fold it lengthways, in exactly the way the savoury *beztel* is folded (see p.20), so that the marzipan is in the centre of a triangle.

Heat the oil in a small saucepan and fry the triangles, two at a time, for 2 minutes.

Meanwhile, in another saucepan, heat the honey until it bubbles. When the *beztels* are ready, drop them into the hot honey for 2 minutes.

Allow to cool before serving.

Nougat de Dattes et Amandes

DATE AND ALMOND NOUGAT

Preparation ✦ 40 minutes
Cooking ✦ 15 minutes
Makes about 30

500 g / 1 lb dates, pitted
125 g / 4 oz almonds
250 g / 8 oz honey
1 tsp ginger
1 tsp sesame seeds
125 g / 4 oz sugar

This is a very sweet and extremely easy way of combining dates and almonds, but it does take a little practice because the caramel syrup hardens quite quickly.

Start by blanching and skinning the almonds following the instructions on p.100, and then grill them for 5 minutes.

Mix the sugar with 25 ml / 1 fl oz of water in a saucepan and heat the until the sugar melts to form a syrup. Mix the syrup with the honey, the dates and the almonds in a large bowl, add the ginger and sesame seeds and quickly shape the mixture into a long snake.

Cut it into slices before it cools – it will harden into a nougat. Serve cold.

Dattes et Noix Fourrées à la Pâte d'Amandes

DATES AND WALNUTS STUFFED WITH MARZIPAN

Preparation ✦ 60-90 minutes
Cooking ✦ 10 minutes for the syrup
Makes 35-40

250 g / 8 oz dates
250 g / 8 oz walnuts, shelled and halved

For the marzipan
250 g / 8 oz almonds
200 g / 7 oz sugar
1 egg
1 tsp orange flower water
A few drops of rum
A variety of natural food colourings

For the glaze
500 g / 1 lb castor sugar
250 ml / 9 fl oz orange flower water

Begin by stoning the dates – take a paring knife and slice open one side so that they can be stuffed.

Then prepare a pound of marzipan following the instructions on p.122. Roll it into a big ball, adding the rum as you do so, and divide it into three or four pieces. Depending on how many different vegetable colours you have, drop a different colour into each piece of marzipan, work it into the paste and then stuff the dates with the marzipan.

With the walnuts, simply put a piece of marzipan between

the two halves and use it to stick them together.

Finally, boil the orange flower water and the sugar together in a saucepan for 5 minutes, until you have a syrup. Dip the stuffed nuts and dates into the syrup for a few seconds to glaze them before putting them on a serving dish.

Fazoulos

FIGEOLA CAKES

Preparation ✦ 40 minutes
Cooking ✦ 5 minutes for each cooking
Makes 30-35

4 eggs
500 g/1 lb flour
1 tsp orange flower water
4 tbsp vegetable oil
4 tbsp water
250 g/8 oz honey or icing sugar for dusting

Whisk the eggs in a large bowl and gradually sift in the flour. Mix well, then add the oil, orange flower water and water. Knead the dough with the palm of your hand until it becomes supple - very much like bread dough – and shape it into a ball.

Stretch the dough as thinly as possible on a floured surface and cut it into pieces approximately 12 inches long and 2 inches wide.

Heat the oil and then carefully pick up each strip of dough – it's very delicate and easily broken – with a fork or spatula and slide it into the oil for a few seconds. It will quickly turn light gold. Dry the cooked *fazoulos* on kitchen paper.

Serve covered either in icing sugar or with warm honey. *Fazoulos* go especially well with mint tea.

Makrodes

ALMOND, DATE AND SEMOLINA CAKES

Preparation ✦ 3 hours
Cooking ✦ 1 hour
Makes about 30

1 kg / 2 lb medium semolina
250 ml / 9 fl oz vegetable oil
200 g / 7 oz dates
Zest of 2 oranges
2 eggs
400 ml / 15 fl oz water
200 g / 7 oz castor sugar
1 tsp salt
250 g / 8 oz clear honey
Vegetable oil for frying

This is a diamond-shaped biscuit that is best made with medium semolina.

Pour the semolina into a saucepan and cook it, dry, over a medium heat, stirring constantly with a wooden spoon until it becomes golden in colour. This should not take more than 7-10 minutes. Transfer the semolina to a big bowl, add 8 fluid ounces of the oil and mix thoroughly. Put to one side for 2 hours.

Then remove the stones from the dates and put them into a food-processor with the remaining 1 fluid ounce of oil and the zest of 2 oranges and make a paste.

When the semolina has sat for 2 hours, add the eggs, the sugar, the water and the salt and mix thoroughly to make a smooth paste. Flatten this with a rolling pin and divide it into two identical strips, each about 2 feet long, 2 inches wide and ½ inch thick.

Spread the date mixture evenly on top of one strip, then carefully lay the second strip on top of that. Pinch the sides so that they close, completely enveloping the date mixture and cut on a diagonal into 1 inch pieces.

Put the honey in a saucepan and warm it on a very low heat. At the same time, put a little oil in another saucepan over a medium heat and drop in the *makrodes* one at a time. Leave them to cook just long enough to become golden brown.

Remove the *makrodes* from the saucepan, dip them in the warm honey and let them cool on a serving dish.

Galettes Sucrées ou Salées

SWEET OR SALTY GALETTES

Preparation ✦ 20 minutes
Cooking ✦ 30 minutes
Makes 25-30

500 g/1 lb flour
200 ml/8 fl oz white wine
200 ml/8 fl oz vegetable oil
150 g/5 oz castor sugar (optional)
50 g/2 oz baking powder
1 tsp sesame seeds
1 tsp aniseed seeds
1 tsp salt

You can make either sweet or salty *galettes* by slightly adapting this simple recipe.

Put the flour in a mixing bowl and gradually mix in the oil, the wine, sugar, baking powder, sesame and aniseed seeds and the salt.

Knead into a dough with the palms of your hands until it softens and is no longer sticky.

Roll out the pastry into a big circle, about $\frac{1}{2}$ inch thick, on a lightly floured surface. Form the circular *galettes* with a pastry-cutter or the rim of a cup about 3 inches in diameter.

Arrange the *galettes* on a baking tray, making sure that first you sprinkle the tray with flour so that the pastry doesn't stick to it, and then prick the top of each *galette* with a fork.

Bake the *galettes* in an oven pre-heated to 180°C/350°F/ gas mark 4 for 20 to 30 minutes, by when they should be a light gold colour.

To make the salty version, make the dough in exactly the same the way but omit the sugar and increase the amount of salt from one teaspoon to one tablespoon.

BREADS

The most popular *pied noir* bread was one we called *le pain courant*. An aniseed-flavoured bread, it was usually baked on Friday mornings to be part of that evening's meal. Many *pieds noirs* still bake it, making the excuse that the home-made variety always tastes better than anything we can buy in the shops, which seems a little odd when one remembers that in France bakery bread is often a wonderful treat and as good as anything you can make at home. But of course there's more to it than just freshness – we bake this bread, like the other dishes which we brought with us from North Africa, as a way of holding onto our past.

Le Pain Courant

EVERYDAY BREAD WITH ANISEED

Preparation ✦ 30 minutes
Cooking ✦ 40 minutes
Makes 2 loaves

500 g / 1 lb plain flour
1 tsp salt
1 tsp aniseed seeds
2 eggs
25 g / 1 oz fresh yeast
250 ml / 9 fl oz warm water

Pour the flour into a large mixing bowl and sprinkle it with salt and the aniseed seeds. Make a well in the centre of the flour, and into that add one beaten egg and then the yeast which you have diluted in the warm water. Mix it very slowly with your fingers until the dough becomes smooth and elastic. It will take you about 10 minutes before you are be able to form a ball with the dough. Divide that in half, then roll each half out by hand on a flour-covered surface, so that both loaves are about a foot in length.

Place the loaves on a board, cover them with a tea-towel and on top of that place a woollen blanket – my mother kept a piece from an old blanket that had long since outlived its usefulness on her bed, and now served only for this. Leave covered for 15–20 minutes.

While the dough is rising, pre-heat the oven to 180°C/ 350°F/gas mark 4. You'll know the dough is ready when it has nearly doubled in size. Transfer it onto a baking tray that you've first sprinkled with flour, scar the top of the loaves with a knife, making three good diagonal cuts, brush the tops with the yolk of the second egg and bake for 40 minutes.

After taking the bread out of the oven, cover it with a tea-towel while it is still warm in order to keep it soft.

Some people always added a little bit of sugar to the dough, to give it a special sweetness, but my mother never added sugar and I still prefer this bread without it.

Le Pain des Jours de Fête

CHOLLA

Preparation ◆ 25 minutes
Cooking ◆ 40 minutes
Makes 2 loaves

500 g / 1 lb plain flour
25 g / 1 oz fresh yeast
250 ml / 9 fl oz warm water
1 tsp salt
2 eggs
2 tsp sesame seeds
50 ml / 2 fl oz vegetable oil
1 tbsp sugar
1 tsp aniseed seeds
1 tsp sesame seeds

This is the bread my mother put on the table for religious holidays, and only on those occasions. She could just as easily have cooked it at any time, and it makes wonderful toast at breakfast-time, but she saved it for holidays, which made both the occasion and the bread itself all the more special.

Put the flour in a large mixing bowl, sprinkle with salt and add the aniseed and sesame seeds. Make a well in the centre of the flour and add the sugar, the yeast, one beaten egg and the oil. Pour in the warm water and mix it slowly with your fingers so that the dough becomes smooth and elastic. As with the *pain courant*, this should take you about 10 minutes.

Form the dough into a ball, divide that ball into two and cut each of them into thirds. Then form each of those thirds into ropes about 1 foot long. Line the three ropes side by side and braid them into a loaf. Repeat the process to make the second loaf.

Place the loaves on a board, cover them with a tea-towel and a piece of old blanket and leave for 15-20 minutes.

Pre-heat the oven to 180°C/350°F/gas mark 4 and, when the dough has nearly doubled in size, transfer it onto a baking tray lightly sprinkled with flour, brush the top of the loaves with the yolk of the second egg and bake for 40 minutes.

Pain Perdu à la Cannelle

PIED NOIR FRENCH TOAST

Preparation ✦ 15 minutes
Cooking ✦ 10 minutes

1 baguette cut into diagonal slices
3 eggs
50 ml/2 oz milk
150 g/5 oz castor sugar
75 g/3 oz butter
1 tbsp cinnamon

This was a Sunday morning breakfast treat made by my father when my mother was sleeping late and a week's accumulation of stale bread had filled the special white canvas bag she always hung in her kitchen to collect old bread.

The stale bread bag was a standard feature in *pied noir* kitchens, and still is in many homes today, not least because we believed the bread had been blessed by God and therefore ought to be used even when stale. Left-over bread often found its way into recipes such as *boulettes de viande au citron* (p.70) and later, when we moved to France, wound up being donated to local fishermen who used it for bait, but for us as children far and away the best use for old bread was in our father's *pain perdu*.

He would start by slicing the bread into small rounds about 1 inch thick, beat the eggs in a bowl, mix in the milk and then thoroughly soak both sides of the bread.

Before frying the bread he would mix the sugar and ground cinnamon together on a plate. Then he melted the butter in a frying pan, added the soaked bread and cooked it over a medium heat until it was golden and crispy on both sides. Using kitchen paper he then transferred the bread to the plate with the sugar and cinnamon and, without allowing the bread to cool, rubbed each slice into it.

My father always serve *pain perdu* to us still warm with milky coffee or mint tea.

Preserves

PRESERVES ARE an important part of our cuisine and we use them in different ways at different meals. Savoury preserves are presented as part of the *kémia*, while sweet preserves are served with afternoon drinks and at tea-time, and can also show up as a dessert or as a jam at breakfast.

You will need hermetically sealed glass jars to make these preserves. These come in many different sizes and are available in most large supermarkets and all good kitchenware shops. All the recipes given here require medium to large jars.

It's important that preserved vegetables are always completely covered with liquid and that, when serving them, a wooden spoon is used, as contact with metal can spoil the vegetables. Preserves are best stored in a cool, dark place and should not be kept for more than six months.

SAVOURY PRESERVES

Piments Rouges en Conserve

RED PEPPERS IN OIL

Preparation ✦ 10 minutes
Preserving ✦ 13 days

20 red peppers
Vegetable oil
Salt

This is one of the preserves that my mother makes all the time. It's not difficult to make and the taste is very distinctive, but you do need to be in a fairly sunny climate because the peppers are dried in the sun, and I have childhood memories of following my mother through the house as she moved a tray of peppers from one window to another to follow the sun.

Begin by grilling the peppers as in the recipe for *frita* (p. 31), then peel them, remove the stems and seeds and wash them under cold water.

Now lay the peppers out on a tray and expose them to the sun, turning them every few hours. You will need to dry them this way for 3 days and, if you're drying them outside, you'll have to bring them inside at night. Don't rush this. The peppers need to be completely dry, and if this takes another day or two in the sun, don't worry.

Once the peppers are dried, sprinkle them with salt, put them in jars, cover with vegetable oil and leave them for 10 days. Serve them with the *kémia*.

Poivrons Verts en Conserve

GREEN PEPPER PRESERVE

Preparation ✦ 10 minutes
Preserving ✦ 10 days

6 large green peppers
White wine vinegar
1 small chilli
3 tbsp salt

Wash the peppers, cut them lengthways into four strips and put them into the jar without removing the stems or the seeds. Cut the chilli into three or four pieces and add it and the salt to the peppers. Then fill the jar with one part of vinegar to three parts of water, seal and leave for 10 days.

The peppers will be ready to eat when they've turned a yellowish colour.

Conserve de Légumes

VEGETABLE PRESERVE

Preparation ✦ 10 minutes
Preserving ✦ 12 days

Half a stick of celery
6 artichoke hearts, cut into quarters
4 carrots, sliced
200 g / 7 oz green olives
Half a cauliflower, cut into small pieces
White wine vinegar
3 tbsp salt

Peel and cut the vegetables, pile them up in the jars and fill half the remaining space with white wine vinegar, half with cold water. Add the salt and leave sealed in the jars for 12 days.

Serve as part of the *kémia*.

Citrons Confits

PRESERVED LEMON FOR COOKING

Preparation ✦ 1 hour
Preserving ✦ 24 days

15-18 lemons, preferably unwaxed
Sea salt
Juice of 2 lemons

Thoroughly wash the lemons, transfer them to a big bowl and cover them with cold water. Soak them for 3 days, changing the water every day.

Remove the lemons from the water and, taking a sharp paring knife, cut into each lemon lengthways four times. Cut the lemons almost as if you were quartering them, and make sure that you dig deeply, almost to the centre, but take care not to not cut right through the lemon as the idea is to keep the lemon intact. Now insert a quarter of a teaspoon of the coarse sea salt into each incision in the lemons.

Place the lemons in sterilised jars — you'll need two — sprinkle each with a tablespoon of sea salt, add the juice of one lemon to each jar and then cover everything with boiling water, filling the jars up to the top. Keep them in a dry place for 3 weeks.

Before cooking with preserved lemons, rinse each one with cold water and cut the peel into small strips. Some *pied noir* families discarded the juice and the pulp, cooking only with the peel, but adding the pulp, juice and the peel to dishes such as *poulet au citron et aux olives* (p. 80) and *poisson sauce chermoula* (p. 96) gives them a tangier flavour.

Citrons Confits Kémia

PRESERVED LEMON APPETISERS

Preparation ✦ 15 minutes
Preserving ✦ 17 days

15 lemons, preferably unwaxed
6 tbsp salt
Juice of 2 lemons
Olive oil

Wash the lemons thoroughly and cut them into thick slices. Put a couple of pinches of salt on top of each slice as you pile them into glass jars. Seal the jars and leave them for 3 days.

The lemon slices will release some juice over the next 3 days, after which you should add the juice of 2 lemons and enough oil to cover the lemons and re-seal the jars.

The lemons will be ready to eat in 2 weeks and are served as part of the *kémia*.

Salade d'Oranges Amères

BITTER ORANGE PRESERVE

Preparation ✦ 45 minutes
Preserving ✦ 7 days

6 bitter oranges
1 onion, finely sliced
3 cloves of garlic, finely chopped
1 tsp mild chilli powder mixed with 5 tbsp vegetable oil
2 tbsp red wine vinegar
200g/7oz Greek black olives
Olive oil

Bitter oranges, known in the English-speaking world as Seville oranges, are used for making marmalade and available only for a short season in January and February. Unfortunately, Sevilles are increasingly hard to find as fewer people make their own marmalade, but they are well worth hunting out for this rather special recipe. This preserve looks a little like chutney and is eaten cold, in small portions, as an accompaniment to grilled meats and fish. I adore it on its own with bread, as a starter.

Peel the bitter oranges so that you take off the outer peel but leave on the thick, white pith. Cut the oranges in halves horizontally, the way you would a grapefruit. Now, finely shred the oranges with a sharp knife, removing the pips as you go, put the pieces of orange into a big bowl and set aside.

Put the finely chopped onion into the bowl with the shredded oranges and add the chilli powder and oil, vinegar and olives, which should not be pitted. Stir the mixture well with a wooden spoon, then transfer to sterilised glass jars, making sure that there is a good layer of oil above the top of the mixture. Seal the jars tightly and put in the fridge for 7 days. Serve cold in small portions and make sure that you keep the preserve refrigerated.

SWEET PRESERVES

Confiture de Coings

QUINCE JAM

Preparation ✦ 20 minutes
Cooking ✦ 1 hour

1 kg / 2 lb quinces
1 tsp cinnamon
1 vanilla pod
750 g / 1½ lb castor sugar

Peel, core and cut the quinces into small pieces.

Put 1 pint of water in a large saucepan together with the sugar, the vanilla and the quinces. Cover and cook over a low heat until the quinces become soft, which should take around 50 minutes.

Stir in the cinnamon, set aside to cool and store in glass jars.

Confiture de Figues Vertes

GREEN FIG JAM

Preparation ✦ 15 minutes
Cooking ✦ 2 hours

2 kg / 4 lb green figs
750 g / 1½ lb castor sugar
1 vanilla pod

Figs make a delicious and surprising jam which is not much made commercially, so it's well worth making this jam when figs are plentiful in the market.

First of all, wash the figs well and remove their stalks.

Put half a pint of water in a large saucepan, add the sugar and heat it over a low flame until the sugar has completely dissolved. Now add the figs, cover the saucepan and simmer gently for 2 hours, during which time you should skim the surface regularly.

The jam will be done when the figs are very tender and tiny bubbles begin to rise from the fruit. When the figs are done, allow them to cool and store in glass jars.

Confiture d'Oranges

ORANGE CONFIT

Preparation ♦ 30 minutes
Cooking ♦ 40 minutes

2 kg / 4 lb navel oranges
2 kg / 4 lb castor sugar
1 lemon

My mother always insists on buying very large oranges with thick skin to make this jam because the skin is easier to grate and you don't cut into the orange, therefore leaving it intact.

Peel the oranges and the lemon and discard their peel. Then soak the fruit in cold water for 1 hour. Bring a large pot of water to the boil, drop in the oranges and the lemon and boil them vigorously for 10 minutes. Then drain the oranges and lemons and, after allowing them to cool slightly, slice them into sixths.

Put 1 pint of water, the sugar and the orange and lemon slices in a saucepan and cook over a medium heat for 30 minutes, skimming the surface from time to time.

Allow the jam to cool and then scoop it all into a glass jar. The result is soft, sweet pieces of fruit in a wonderful syrup that pulls apart like angel hair. Serve it with tea or as a dessert.

Drinks

DESPITE BEING FRENCH, and despite the fact that some good wines are made in Morocco, we *pieds noirs* have never been considered serious wine-drinkers. A bottle of Bordeaux might make an appearance on the table on special occasions, but not in the way that wine does in most French homes, as an obligatory accompaniment to a meal. One reason is that the colonial authorities never encouraged wine-drinking in Muslim Morocco. Another perhaps more important consideration is that wine is not well suited to such a hot climate.

What we did drink, and still enjoy, is *anisette* or pastis. There was a time when everybody made their own, but nowadays everyone buys the commercial varieties and a bottle appears automatically with the *kémia*. Two other drinks which were often served with the *kémia* were *mahia* and *borha*. The former is an eau de vie made from dates and fennel, the latter a fig liqueur. Both are made commercially, easily found in France and increasingly to be had in Middle Eastern food shops elsewhere in Europe as well as in North America.

Because the climate encouraged it, outdoor cafés were very much a part of our life in North Africa. Adults would meet friends there, taking *le kawa* – Turkish coffee – after lunch, or an *anisette* with some *kémia* after work. But for those of us who were then too young for alcohol, a visit to a café meant *aqua limon*. On hot afternoons, or sometimes as a special treat after dinner, my father would take us for a cool glass of lemonade.

Aqua Limon

LEMONADE

Preparation ✦ 20 minutes

2 lemons, preferably unwaxed
125 g / 4 oz castor sugar

Wash and zest the lemons. Boil the zest in half a pint of water for 5 minutes and then allow it to sit for 10 minutes.

Meanwhile, cut the lemons in half and extract their juice.

Now dissolve the sugar in 2 pints of warm water, mix in the boiled zest and its liquid, the syrup and the lemon juice.

Strain the mixture into a bottle and stand it in your freezer until ice crystals start to form. Just before the juice begins to freeze, take the bottle out of the freezer, stir the juice and serve.

Thé à la Menthe

MINT TEA

Preparation ✦ 10 minutes

A bunch of fresh mint
1 tbsp green tea or Chinese gunpowder tea
10 cubes sugar

Mint tea is without doubt the most famous of Moroccan drinks and tea-drinking is every bit as much of an institution in that part of the world as it is in England.

There are two tricks to making mint tea – using very fresh mint and putting the sugar directly into the teapot.

Begin by rinsing the teapot with boiling water, vigorously swishing the water around to clean and pre-heat the pot. Discard that water and then add the green tea, sugar cubes, fresh mint and, finally, freshly boiling water to the warm teapot. Leave it to infuse for 5 minutes.

Moroccans drink mint tea from small glasses rather than the cups to which we are accustomed in Europe. They – and we – pour the tea with the teapot close to the glass at first and then, as the tea pours, raise it higher and higher. This makes no difference whatsoever to the flavour of the tea and, until you become skilled at pouring tea like this, can be rather messy. It does, however, add to the sense of ceremony and I suppose that is why we were happy to borrow this habit, like so many others, from our Arab neighbours.

Index

An independent publishing house, Serif publishes a wide range of international fiction and non-fiction.

If you would like to receive a copy of our current catalogue, please write to:

Serif
47 Strahan Road
London E3 5DA

or

1489 Lincoln Avenue
St Paul
MN 55105

or

c/o Wakefield Press
PO Box 2266
Kent Town
South Australia 5071

or you can visit our website at
http://www.serif.demon.co.uk/

✦ *also published by Serif* ✦

Traditional Moroccan Cooking

RECIPES FROM FEZ

Madame Guinaudeau

Foreword by Claudia Roden

Moroccan cuisine is famous for its subtle blending of spices, herbs and honey with meat and vegetables. In Fez, the country's culinary centre, the cooking has numerous influences – Arab and Berber, with hints of Jewish, African and French. The country's classic dishes are the famous *couscous*, *tagines* or stews, and *bistilla*, an exquisite pie made with a flaky pastry.

Capturing the atmosphere of Fez, cultural capital of the medieval Moorish world, Madame Guinaudeau takes us behind closed doors into the kitchens and dining rooms of the old city. She invites us to a banquet in a wealthy home, shopping in the spice market and to the potter's workshop; shares with us the secrets of preserving lemons for a *tagine*; shows us how to make Moroccan bread.

Traditional Moroccan Cooking is the perfect introduction to a splendid culinary heritage and a vivid description of an ancient and beautiful city. It offers a taste of the delights to be found in one of the world's great gastronomic centres.

'Successfully evokes the magic flavours of Fez'
Nigel Slater, *The Observer*

'Wonderful descriptions of the food and how to cook it'
Thane Prince, *Daily Telegraph*

paperback